BE RESILIENT

HOW TO BUILD A STRONG TEENAGE MIND FOR TOUGH TIMES

NICOLA MORGAN

WALKER
BOOKS

To Wyn, Bethan and Megan, heroes of resilience,
with love.

First published 2021 by Walker Books Ltd,
87 Vauxhall Walk, London SE11 5HJ

2 4 6 8 10 9 7 5 3 1

© 2021 Nicola Morgan

The right of Nicola Morgan to be identified as author of
this work has been asserted by her in accordance with the
Copyright, Designs and Patents Act 1988

This book has been typeset in Eureka Sans Pro

Printed in Great Britain by CPI Group (UK) Ltd, Croydon,
CR0 4YY

British Library Cataloguing in Publication Data: a catalogue
record for this book is available from the British Library

ISBN 978-1-4063-9925-7

www.walker.co.uk

MIX
Paper from
responsible sources
FSC® C020471

CONTENTS

■▷ INTRODUCTION

It's one of the hardest facts of life that every human must learn: bad things can happen. From small upsets or disappointments to major, life-changing distresses, they can happen to anyone, whether we "deserve" them or not, and we don't know when or what they will be. Our challenge is to know this and yet not live in fear, not ruin every happy moment by dwelling on bad things that might – but might not – be round the corner. Because wonderful things happen, too! We have to be realistic and ready, but positive and confident in our ability to stay strong. That's resilience.

Our lives are like an ocean and we are the small boat trying to cross safely. Sometimes the water is calm and we sail easily, without a care in the world. But storms can come, sometimes out of a blue sky. The storms can be small and brief or long and treacherous. Just as some parts of the ocean are more dangerous than others, some parts of our lives are more difficult. And not all oceans are the same, just as some people's lives have more challenges than others.

Teenage years are often particularly rocky. Younger children can face challenges, too, but it's easier for adults to reassure or distract them and they often feel secure in the knowledge that their adults can sort things out.

But you, an adolescent, are not so easily reassured. You've learnt that no one can be entirely safe from harm and life cannot be risk-free; you've noticed that good and innocent people can have sadness or disaster; you might have experienced it yourself. Your teenage brain allows you to understand big concepts, to discuss topics such as war, disease, death, suicide, abuse and injustice – and you need to be allowed to have those discussions, even though they can be frightening and painful.

Adolescence can be exciting but it can also be scary. You might

7 ⚡

not have the reassuring comfort of adults and now you're trying to work out how to find your way without the support young people deserve. When I was a teenager, we were in the Cold War, which coloured my fears. I had horrible war-related dreams and I needed my parents to reassure me, to put my fears in context and to tell me that all would *probably* be well. And they needed to push my mind in optimistic directions, towards success, knowledge, work, the things I could control rather than the things I couldn't. That helped me build resilience, though resilience was not a word that was much used.

You might be worried about terrorism or illness: as I write this we are living through the COVID-19 outbreak that began in 2020 and our lives are dramatically affected by various restrictions and lockdowns and all the worries associated with the virus. Maybe you have other worries, too: something going on in your family, or with a friend, or your schoolwork. You could have small fears or big fears but they can all seem big at the time, especially because, while we are in any particular crisis, we don't *know* what the outcome will be.

If we are the boat on the ocean of our life, we need to be built strongly enough to withstand storms – small or big – that we can't foresee. Not only built well but looked after, repaired and strengthened regularly.

We must learn not only to navigate the bad weather but also to repair any damage after each battering wave. And perhaps to come back stronger, so that we are even better able to deal with the next one. Humans are learning creatures, adapting and using what we've learnt to become stronger, fitter, healthier. That's great resilience.

Life isn't just about surviving bad things, though: it's also about pleasure, success, appreciation, fulfilment, purpose, excitement. If all we are doing is being prepared for possible negatives, we'll miss the actual positives. If survival means feeling constantly anxious, unconfident, ready for disaster, that's not really living.

In short, we need to build resilient bodies and minds, create in ourselves the strength to withstand any storms but also to bounce back and enjoy the calm rhythms and the sunlight glinting off the water. That's living well. That's being brilliantly resilient.

I can't know what challenges you face now and no one knows what is round the corner for you. Sometimes, you'll have your family or friends or trusted adults to support you and share your challenges; at other times, you might be more alone. Sometimes everyone around you will be experiencing a difficult time together, though it will always be slightly different for each individual. Sometimes you might have something bad going on inside your own head, perhaps accompanied by dark thoughts you deal with alone at night. But whatever these difficulties, whether personal or shared, whether short-lived or lingering, whether small or huge, the resilience you can grow now will help you get through and also give you the strength to face forward and welcome all the wonderful things in your future with optimism and bravery and hope. To put fears in perspective and not let them spoil your life.

Be Resilient offers you the practical tools to build a truly resilient life, with both your mind and body.

In this book, you will find:

- ♥ All about what resilience is.
- ♥ Five areas of your life where you can build your resilience: your support network, skills, coping strategies, courage and future.
- ♥ Practical activities to build each of those areas.
- ♥ Fictional characters who are struggling with resilience, for

you to think about and empathise with. You might identify with them yourself.

♥ Reflection activities so you can say how you'd help those characters – and you'll find my suggested responses, too.

♥ Diary activities – things you can, if you wish, record in a notebook or diary to help you see how you're building your resilience. You could buy or find a beautiful notebook, or just open a new document on your computer or use an app on your phone. You can obviously write anything you want in your diary – it's for your eyes only – but I will give you some prompts and ideas at the end of each chapter.

All the ideas and practical tools in this book will help you be more in control when times are tough and you feel anxious or overwhelmed. If you can learn all this now, you'll be able to use the techniques throughout your life, becoming mentally stronger, building resilience. You'll enjoy life more, too.

Becoming more resilient is a brilliantly positive, useful and fulfilling goal. This book is here to show you how you can achieve that goal. You can survive those tough times and thrive!

CHAPTER ONE:
UNDERSTANDING RESILIENCE

WHAT IS RESILIENCE?

Resilience literally means "the ability to rebound or bounce back". It comes from a Latin word – resilire, meaning "to bounce back" – and has been used since the seventeenth century. But for the first couple of hundred years it was only used to refer to objects, describing whether they could bounce or spring back to their original shape after being stretched or bent. Today when we talk about an object being resilient, we refer to how well it stands up to or recovers from various attacks. Some types of stone or wood are more resilient to water than others; some plants are resilient to frost or drought and others are not. The word wasn't used to describe people until the nineteenth century.

When we talk about people being resilient, we mean they have the ability to bounce back after a problem or setback; to recover their confidence and optimism so that they can face the future positively.

The problem or setback could be illness (mental or physical), distress and sadness, fear, loss of money or job, criticism or failure. It could be small, such as getting a low mark in a test or being told off; or big, such as failing to achieve something that you'd worked hard at for years, or breaking up with a friend; or even bigger, such as being abused or dealing with the death of someone close. Different people will feel each of these problems in their own way, depending on many circumstances: for example, when parents split up, this can be a worse experience for some people than others. Any upsetting experience you can think of will not be felt in the same way by everyone.

We also talk about communities being resilient. A family might need to bounce back after a loss of income or a death or serious illness. A company might need to be resilient against financial recession or rent or taxes going up. A school might need to be resilient after a tragic event happening to someone in it. Your group of friends could be resilient if, for example, you don't fall apart when you have an argument or upset. (On the other hand, it's also quite natural for friendship groups to separate and change over time so this is not a judgement.)

This book is about you and your resilience. I'm sure you have already experienced setbacks of some sort. Some of you will have had some really difficult things to deal with. You might feel you've coped well or you might feel very fragile and perhaps frightened about bad things happening again. Everyone is different in the challenges they have experienced, the support they have around them and how they feel when they think about problems that might be ahead. Everyone has different levels of anxiety and amounts of existing resilience, different pasts, presents and futures. None of that is your "fault" but this book will help you overcome any problems you might have had and feel stronger for the future.

One thing about humans is that *everything* changes us. We will never be *exactly* the same after an event as we were before. So being resilient doesn't mean bouncing back to being precisely the same as you were: it means being just as strong or even stronger than before. It often means accepting change and seeing it as growth: "I dealt with that – it was hard but I learnt something about myself from it and I know I can deal with tough things now."

This book will show you how to do that, in practical ways that you can use throughout your life, whatever age you are.

OTHER WORDS FOR RESILIENT

When I was investigating the word "resilient", I came across lots of synonyms – words that mean the same – and I thought you might like to see some of them. They will set you off feeling positive about resilience, which sounds quite a dull word!

Springy, bouncy, elastic, flexible, rubbery, stretchy, whippy, supple, strong, adaptable, irrepressible, hardy, quick to recover, stretchable, pliable, tough.

Which is your favourite? I like irrepressible, which literally means "you can't keep me down".

IS RESILIENCE A FIXED PERSONALITY TRAIT?

Most psychologists – experts in human behaviour – now believe that resilience is not a fixed aspect of personality and that we can learn to be more resilient. Although it sometimes looks as though some people just are naturally more resilient than others, this is not true. Resilience may be *easier* for some people than for others, for various reasons.

Your resilience may be different from someone else's at this moment because of factors such as:

- ♥ Whether lots of negative things or lots of positive things have happened in your life.
- ♥ Whether the negative things feel as though they've dominated your life – or there's been one big negative thing that you haven't been able to shake off.
- ♥ How the adults around you helped you process negative experiences.
- ♥ Whether the adults in your life display resilience themselves.

♥ Whether the adults in your life have shown you that you
can make good choices and that those choices will make a
difference – or whether you've learnt that you have no control
and everything must be done for you and happen to you.

Those factors, which you have no control over, can affect your
mindset. For example, they might make you tend to explain bad
events through a self-blaming, negative, fatalistic filter ("It's my
fault or I'm just an unlucky person") rather than with a positive
attitude ("Well, that happened – how can I deal with it?").

How you *explain* your experiences in your head can affect your
resilience. This is because resilience is in your mind and your
mind contains language. The thoughts you have and the way you
talk to yourself make a difference to how you feel and how you
feel makes a difference to how you act. Thinking, feeling and
acting are all tied together. So the words you use in your head –
your thoughts – make a difference.

However, personality can also play a part in how easy or hard
it is to be resilient. For example, if you are by nature a worrier,
you might dwell more on negative situations. Or, if you are
a particularly caring or sensitive person, you might be more
affected by distressing events than someone else and therefore
could have a more difficult task to overcome them.

On the other hand, lots of people would argue that many
"personality traits" are things we have developed and learnt,
rather than them being fixed and inborn. For example, a person
might develop perfectionist tendencies after watching a parent
behave like that; or after experiencing praise when doing
something very well and wanting that praise again; or seeing
an older sibling praised for an achievement that the younger
one can't manage; or after hearing unintended messages about
perfection from the adults around them, or on television or
social media.

Human behaviours are caused by *many* things, including emotions, temptations, biological instincts or reflexes, behaviours of the people we see, events that happen to us, and aspects of our personalities that we have either been born with or developed during our lives up to this moment.

Resilience is affected by all of these things but most experts believe that personality plays only a part. In your life so far, other influences have already led you to develop certain amounts of resilience, either more or less compared to other people you know. And you can develop more.

Some people use the phrase "character-building" when they talk about difficult childhood experiences. This is a dangerous viewpoint because it sounds as though it justifies harsh treatment of children. It doesn't! The fact that many children who had difficult childhoods become strong, undamaged adults does not mean it's a good thing. Other children with difficult childhoods *are* negatively affected as adults. We should not have to have horrible things happen to us in order to become strong individuals. Yes, a few knocks and scrapes should cause no lasting harm and may make us stronger and more skilful for the rest of our life, but some knocks and scrapes leave scars, mentally or physically.

Resilience is about creating a mind that is strong and ready and undamaged, strengthened for the future.

Whatever the truth of how personality affects resilience, it doesn't alter this: that resilience can be learnt, grown, improved, built. Whatever your starting point, however unresilient you believe yourself to be, however badly you have been affected by difficult experiences, you can become better at bouncing back after problems and even become stronger.

It's great news that resilience is not a fixed personality trait. Whoever you are and whatever your past life and your situation now, you *can* grow more resilience. This book will show you how!

WHY MIGHT SOME PEOPLE HAVE LESS RESILIENCE?

Several factors can make resilience more challenging. They won't make it impossible but it's just like starting a race further back than other people. If some of these things apply to you, don't *worry* (because this book will show you how to overcome problems), but use the knowledge as a way of being kind to yourself. None of these things is your fault. But you might need extra support and you might need to try harder than people with easier situations.

- **A difficult start in life** – This is sometimes described as "adverse childhood experience" and it covers a wide range of situations, including parental illness, neglect, trauma, abuse or any set of factors that meant your earliest months and years were particularly hard. If you were adopted or fostered at an early age, you might well have had difficult times before that, even before you were old enough to know. This *might* affect your mindset and anxiety later so it's helpful to be aware.

- **Death of someone close** – A loss of one or both parents or main carers; or the loss of a sibling or other close family member.

- **Mental illnesses** – It's more difficult to be mentally resilient if you have a history of anxiety disorders or any mental illnesses, and it can be harder if the people around you do, too, as you may take on some of their anxiety.

- **Repeated distresses** – Although some people become stronger when they suffer several bad luck events, others naturally find themselves worn down. Distress is exhausting and it is understandable that some people start to assume that bad things will happen to them and feel very anxious about that.

- ♥ **Lack of support** – We all need people to rely on and support us when things are tough. If you don't feel that you have trusted adults who are properly there for you and that you can turn to, you might find your resilience shrinks.

- ♥ **Lack of good role models** – If the adults you live with don't demonstrate resilience themselves, it is likely that this will rub off on you and that you will find it harder to be resilient yourself. I am not blaming the adults in this case: there are lots of understandable reasons why an adult might be unresilient, especially if they haven't had the benefit of strong advice in a book like this or received good support themselves.

Two other factors can have a negative effect. I have separated them from the above list partly because they are so common and partly because they feel like a different category from the more negative experiences I have already mentioned:

- ♥ **Too much parental help** – When parents worry so much that they don't let their children take risks and face challenges, this can mean that the child grows up feeling too anxious themselves and can't bear failure or setback.

- ♥ **Certain personality traits such as perfectionism and fear of failure** – These can mean that every small setback feels enormous and the person finds it hard to move on and try again. This is very common.

Very many people will find that at least one of those factors applies to them. But problems do not have to drag you down. Or, when they do, resilience helps you pull yourself back up! You're going to learn how in this book.

OTHER IMPORTANT WORDS

Resilience isn't the only important word. Here are some other concepts which I'll use in this book. You will be familiar with the words but I want to make clear exactly what I mean by them.

SELF-ESTEEM OR CONFIDENCE?

These sound like similar traits but are not identical. They are both positive words, both describing a state of mind where a person feels good about themselves. They are both important, too, and when a person has low self-esteem or low confidence it can weaken their resilience.

But confidence is the more important and the broader of the two because confidence looks forward. Feeling confident means feeling and believing that you can do something, that you have the skills and resources to face what you have to face.

Self-esteem is more about what you think of yourself, whether you think you're a valuable person. Self-esteem is all about you and your worth; confidence is about how you can affect your future and the world around you.

A person can be overconfident, perhaps taking dangerous risks, so confidence does need to be based on some wisdom and common sense, too. A person could also have self-esteem so high that it becomes arrogance, narcissism, cockiness, so self-esteem needs to be balanced by sensitivity.

So, you can see that self-esteem and confidence are similar but not exactly the same. You need the right amount of both, but confidence is the one I'd love to see you display most of. Confidence is the one this book will help you build. The result of that is likely to be better self-esteem, too. Double win!

HAPPINESS, WELL-BEING AND MENTAL HEALTH

These are three more ideas that are similar but not the same.

Happiness is an emotion. It describes a noticeable and immediate sense of joy or contentment. "Joy" is an intense, exciting type of happiness, such as you might have when you see someone you love, or you win a prize, or someone gives you a present you really like. "Contentment" is a calmer sense of happiness, such as you might feel when you sit outside in the sunshine or go for a walk somewhere that's special to you.

Well-being is not an immediate emotion but a longer state of existence where you have good mental and physical health, you feel strong and able to face the day. You are neither too stressed nor too bored. You feel positive about today, the week and the future. You feel good about your life – or at least not bad. You might feel actual happiness at the same time or you might say "I feel fine – I'm OK".

Mental health is also not an emotion; it is similar to well-being. I've noticed a lot of people say "mental health" when they mean "mental illness". (Mental *illness* is when you have a specific psychological ailment, such as a form of depression, or an anxiety disorder, or a severe phobia, or an eating disorder.) I've also heard people say "I have mental health", but we all have mental health: some of us have good mental health and some have poor mental health. People with "poor mental health" include both people with specific mental illnesses and people who often feel that their mental state is fragile or low but they don't have a diagnosable mental illness.

Well-being and mental health are closely linked. If you have good well-being you will also tend to have good mental health. You still might have a specific mental challenge or vulnerability but your positive well-being will help you deal with it.

Well-being and good mental health are linked to resilience in two directions: building resilience will improve well-being and mental health; and when you have good well-being and mental health it is easier to be resilient.

So, this book will help your well-being *and* mental health. In turn, that will help your performance and success in whatever you try to do. And that will increase your happiness. Which will also boost your resilience. Excellent!

WHAT ARE THE INGREDIENTS OF RESILIENCE?

There are skills and characteristics we need if we are going to become as resilient as possible, ready for whatever the future throws at us and to make the most of all the wonderful things life can offer.

Different psychologists have focused on different words for these characteristics and come up with different ways of presenting them. You might hear people talk about the need for grit and determination, motivation, purposefulness, ambition, self-belief, aspiration, connectedness, learning, confidence, generosity, mindfulness, gratitude and more. Too many words!

I think the reason why there are so many different ways of describing the ingredients of resilience is that resilience is a whole way of living and thinking. It's about how you look at everything that happens to you and every thought that enters your head. It's about how you make your mind work. And that's hard to break down into small and simple pieces.

But I've done it, after a great deal of thinking! I'm going to give you five areas of your life to build and strengthen. Everyone can do this, whether their resilience is currently weak or strong. These are aspects of your life that will not only give you resilience but all the other character strengths that strong minds have.

In *Be Resilient*, I'm going to show you how to build your:

1. Support network.
2. Skills.
3. Coping strategies.
4. Courage.
5. Future.

You can do this!

Now that you know what resilience is and you believe that you can improve yours and feel stronger as you go through your life, let's look at the ways in which you can start to build that resilience. They are not things you need to tackle one by one, or focus on one on a Monday and another on a Tuesday. They are ways of thinking and living that will come into every day of your life. Each day, you'll find opportunities to put these ideas into action and every time you do you'll be helping to make yourself stronger, more resilient.

Each of the chapters that follow will start by asking you to imagine some characters. They are not actual people but they are certainly based on characteristics of realistic human beings. You might recognise some as being like people you know and some will probably be like you, too. When I describe these people, I'm not being judgemental. I am offering examples of different personalities, situations and behaviours that will show you ways in which you yourself might grow resilience. We can learn from other people: from their mistakes as well as their successes. Seeing examples of typical humans and how they face what happens to them gives us both empathy and self-knowledge, two things that are very important as we navigate our lives.

Near the end of each chapter, there'll be a Reflection Activity that asks you to think about the characters again now you've learnt so much about the topic. What would you say to those people to help them build resilience? Are there things they can do to make their lives and experiences more positive? What have you learnt from them? How could you be a good friend to those people? And in the Appendix (on page 176), you'll find my own suggested answers to those questions.

THE HAPPIEST MAN ON EARTH

One hundred years old in 2020, a survivor of Buchenwald and Auschwitz Nazi concentration camps, Eddie Jaku is a supreme example of resilience. He came through those dreadful experiences with a promise he made to himself: to smile every day. *The Happiest Man on Earth* is the title of his autobiography, which tells the story of how he managed to build the immense mental strength he needed.

Eddie knows that a great deal of luck played its part in his physical survival and he knows so well how many other brave, strong and wonderful people did not survive. But his story shows us the potential of human minds to overcome "bad things". Most of us will, fortunately, never experience anything remotely as bad as he did, but we will all have our own challenges and dark times and we can learn from Eddie and other resilient people.

It was while I was writing this book that I heard Eddie interviewed on the BBC and I found his story inspirational. I felt it was very relevant to what I was writing for you.

His vow to smile every day: could something as simple as that make a difference? He says, "Happiness is something we can choose." It's not always that easy but I think we can choose to smile and we can choose to try to build our resilience. For some people, in some situations, it's harder than for others. But Eddie was an ordinary teenager when he made this choice to be happy. He did it. I believe you can.

DIARY TIME

Writing a diary can be a powerful way to sort out and clarify your thoughts, as well as being a great record of your progress. You don't have to follow any rules of writing, as this is only for yourself and will not be judged by other people. And you don't have to do it at all!

Here are some things you could record in your diary now:

1. Which are your three favourite words from the "Other words for resilient" section on page 13?
2. What are you hoping to get out of this book?
3. What do you feel are the biggest challenges you face at the moment? Is there anything undermining your self-esteem and confidence?
4. When did you last feel happy? Can you write about what that felt like?
5. How resilient do you feel? Do you think you cope quite well when difficult things happen? What types of problem do you find most difficult?
6. Can you think of a time when you tried hard even though you worried that you wouldn't be able to succeed? What happened?

CHAPTER TWO:
BUILD YOUR SUPPORT NETWORK

HOW DOES THIS HELP RESILIENCE?

The people in our lives can help or hinder our resilience. Some of our connections will help us grow strong and others will drag us down. Being alone drags us down, too, so the key is to build good, positive relationships. That's how humans work best. Luckily, there are things we can do to make sure that we have positive connections, people we can turn to when necessary, people who care about us – and whom, in turn, we care about and support. This chapter shows you why these people are so important to resilience and how you can make your support network the best it can be.

TEENAGE EXAMPLES

Take a look at these characters. They all have people who are on their side and could support them but they might not see this. They might not be valuing or using their support network and there might be things they could do so that the people who care about them can help them become stronger.

♥ ♥ ♥

Abbie is in her second year of secondary school. She's always been quiet and shy and worries a lot about what people think. Lots of kids in her year group hang out in noisy groups and she feels excluded; occasionally someone will tease her and a couple of times they've said something about her being boring. Because she doesn't want to join in activities, her parents don't push her into after-school clubs, and they're busy with their jobs anyway so they're just happy that she doesn't seem to be having schoolwork problems. She doesn't have brothers or sisters. In primary school, Abbie had a good friend called Bilal and they used to spend a lot of time outside, collecting bugs, making nature videos and writing stories, but when they started secondary school Bilal was teased about hanging out with "that boring girl" and they're not friends any more. Abbie is happiest reading books, drawing and making videos – she's very creative. She helps the school librarian at lunchtimes to avoid her noisy year group. There are always a few students from her year there, too, but when Abbie has tentatively tried to engage with them they haven't really responded. The other day a new girl asked Abbie to come back to her house to do homework but Abbie felt uncertain so she said no.

Abbie is feeling more and more anxious. Everyone's growing up and she feels different from them all: quieter, more boring, childish, less fashionable. She has dreams where she's the only person alive who speaks her language or she's alone on a beach the size of a desert or she's the only person on a plane and she has to fly it. Sometimes she thinks she might be going mad: the thoughts in her head seem so out of control. Why is she different from everyone else? Why are they growing up and she's stuck as a child? What is wrong with her?

♥ ♥ ♥

Chris is in his fifth year at a huge London secondary school, a few months from the most important exams of his life, which he's set to ace. He's the middle of three children, with a brother two years older and sister four years younger. His parents split up ages ago and Chris never sees his father. His mother remarried recently and Chris is not close to his stepdad. His mother is now pregnant and it's a difficult pregnancy. Chris's older brother is hostile to him: Chris is a very good student but his brother is not and is getting into a lot of trouble at school. His sister is fixated on getting into a particular school and is receiving private tuition and taking a lot of attention. Chris's mum and stepdad have their hands full. But Chris is causing no trouble and wants to keep it that way.

One evening his mother is taken into hospital as an emergency; his sister goes to their grandparents' house; Chris and his brother stay at home. Except that his brother doesn't: he stays out all night, comes back dishevelled and wide-eyed but refusing to say what's happened; Chris has to cover for him to his stepdad. After a sleepless night of worry, Chris hands in poor homework and does badly in a test for the first time ever. When a teacher asks why, he can't find the words. He can't concentrate on classes and disappoints two more teachers. Classmates tease him: Chris, the class swot, in trouble! He has a couple of good friends, also top students, but he can't explain what's happening to them. He can't really explain it to himself. Over the next week, with his mother still in hospital, his brother swearing him to secrecy about his night-time escapades, and his stepdad focusing on his own fears, Chris's life spirals down. He can't concentrate on schoolwork and revision is out of the window.

He starts to panic. Maybe his success was all a charade? Maybe he's not really cut out for the world of business he was aiming for? Maybe he's not going to ace his exams and be on track for a good university after all? And who does he have to turn to for help?

♥ ♥ ♥

Seema is fourteen and super-popular: lucky in looks, health, body, brains, money, friends. Or so it seems. But some people are starting to notice that she's losing weight. They're commenting on it, too, which Seema loves. When her parents say she's too thin, that's a compliment, especially as they used to say that her chubbiness would disappear once she started to grow up. When her friends comment on her small waist or thin arms, it makes her feel excited in her stomach. She keeps pinching herself, checking that there's less fat than yesterday. She doesn't see herself as thin, or even slim, but she loves other people saying it.

Now some friends are talking like her parents, saying she's too thin, that there's something wrong with her. That she should get help. They're just jealous, she thinks. They're not her real friends, are they? Her real friends are the people who help her eat less and less, aren't they? Because real friends help you do what you want, don't they?

Seema doesn't know it but she is dangerously ill. She has a completely wrong view of who her real friends are. She thinks she's strong and in control because she can manage not to eat but she's not strong, not resilient, and somehow she needs to find her real friends and listen to them.

Abbie, Chris and Seema are each in a situation which could become worse or better. Those are very useful times to build resilience! If they can take certain actions now, they can overcome the current problems and use that success to feel more resilient for future similar situations.

They are each having a difficult time for different reasons. The reasons are not their fault but there are things they can do to make it better. Abbie, Chris and Seema, and many like them, have people who could support them but they either aren't seeing that or they aren't making use of their supporters. They are taking too much on themselves and they believe they are

27

alone. This means their resilience is threatened, because when bad things happen they may be knocked down and not reach for a helping hand to pull them back up.

There are many other situations, personalities and reasons why someone might have problems finding, building or knowing their supporters, their team. But there are ways we can all make sure we have the people we need to help us, whether we are like Seema, Chris or Abbie or any other individual. We don't know much about Bilal from Abbie's story, only that he felt that his new group of friends was preferable to spending time with Abbie. It's quite possible that he was doing the right thing for himself so we shouldn't condemn him: friendships do change and we need to be able to go with our instincts.

You probably know people like those in the examples. You may identify with parts of their situations yourself. Or you may be completely different and have entirely different problems. Whoever you are and whatever your situation, you need other people. "No man is an island" said the poet John Donne. Bearing in mind that this is "man" in the sense of "human", you might like to see a bit more of the poem:

"No man is an island entire of itself; every man
is a piece of the continent, a part of the main;
... any man's death diminishes me,
because I am involved in mankind."

We are involved in each other; we can't be separate; or, if we are, we are weaker. *Building your support network* sounds a bit contrived and cold, though, doesn't it? Making friends isn't something we're supposed to do deliberately; surely it's just a natural human way of being? We don't need lessons in it, do we?

Perhaps we sometimes do. When things are going well, it's easy to make new friends naturally, have fun with people, choose whether to join in things or be on our own. But when things are going badly or we're not feeling so great about ourselves (which is when we most need resilience), we can make mistakes, get things wrong, not find human contact easy, or not know who to turn to.

Here are some problems we might have:

- ❤ We might retreat into ourselves and cut ourselves off because sometimes being alone is easier.
- ❤ We might be so overwhelmed by our problems that we feel that no one can help.
- ❤ We might turn to the wrong friends. Some friends are good when things are going well but not so good in a crisis.
- ❤ Our friends might not be able to help because they have their own problems.
- ❤ We might not be thinking straight and might not know who is the best person to turn to.
- ❤ We might not want to tell personal stuff and innermost thoughts to someone close to us.
- ❤ We might be a quiet and reserved type of person.
- ❤ We might lack confidence and not believe that our friends will *want* to help us.
- ❤ We might have serious problems at home and not want to share them.

So, for lots of reasons, and especially when things are tough, we might need help with building the strongest possible support networks. It's not a weakness or character flaw if you need that help. It is also likely that you already have a much better support network than you think. You just haven't noticed it or seen what it can do.

Whether you are similar to Abbie, Chris, Seema or none of them, let's investigate the importance of support networks and how to build the best ones we can.

WHY ARE SUPPORT NETWORKS SO IMPORTANT?

Humans are social creatures by nature. This means that we are drawn to live and work in groups: individuals connected to other individuals in different ways. These connections are bonds of family, friendship or of working together. These bonds can be both created and broken. Even if a person lives on their own, even if they are home-schooled, even if someone has a job that means they work on their own – like me – they are still linked to others. There are very rare people who choose to live entirely cut off from all human contact and it's possible to imagine that there are people who have been cut off by circumstance. The story of Robinson Crusoe imagines this, for example. But this is very unusual and not how humans have evolved to be. It is *extremely* rarely a choice we make, although it's quite common for us to need to be alone *sometimes*.

Being so social – and having larger networks than other social species such as apes and dogs – is part of why humans have succeeded so well. Modern humans – *Homo sapiens* – date back 200,000 years ago and beyond, when we were all "hunter-gatherers". We survived and thrived because we lived in groups, helping and protecting each other. We were more successful hunters when we hunted as a team; we were safer from predators if we lived and raised our children in groups; and we became successful at building, creating, problem-solving, farming, making tools and travelling because we shared information with each other and worked collaboratively. We shared knowledge with the people we had a connection with. And the more connections we had, the more we could share and the more we could help and be helped.

Evolution wires our brains so that we are attracted to do things which help us either survive or succeed – or both. And being social helps us both survive and succeed. So, we are biologically wired to be social and, when we can't be, that's a problem for us.

All this applies today: although we can have ideas on our own (and many people like doing that), we also *all* benefit from the sharing of ideas and from listening to other people's thoughts or information. We can share and listen through books or screens rather than face to face, and there are advantages to both, but a face-to-face conversation often makes it easier to spark ideas and thoughts and feelings that are strong and important and vivid.

Modern technology does allow us to live and work with less face-to-face contact and many more people live alone than used to one hundred years ago. But we are still able to be connected in many ways to lots of different people. Some people need this more than others but we all need to know that someone, somewhere, is there for us and that we can turn to them if we need or want to.

We need friends at all times but we need them especially when we are down or suffering. Isolation is a strong triggering factor for mental illnesses such as depression and anxiety disorders. Isolation is not good for resilience.

I live in a small village. I moved there with my husband a few years ago, knowing no one. If my husband and I had chosen to keep to ourselves, relying solely on our family and old friends and not bothering to make new ones, we would not now be able to call on people locally if one of us was ill or needed help or felt lonely. We didn't make new friends because we wanted to have people to help us, of course. We made new friends because we like making friends and because we (people) are *wired* to do that. It's not contrived or deliberate. It's natural and heart-warming and fun. But for many people it's not easy, so sometimes we do have to be a bit deliberate about it: we sometimes need to say to ourselves, "I don't really feel like going to that party because I won't know anyone, but I will do it because I might meet an interesting person and have fun."

So, friends and support networks – whatever you like to call them – are important for our survival, our success and our mental health. Because we are human and that's how humans are wired to be. And humans are wired to be like that because being social brings benefits.

Let's look at how to build that support network to help your resilience when things go wrong or if things are already going wrong.

COMPASSION – BE YOUR OWN SUPPORTER

Soon I'm going to ask you to think about who is already in your support network but I can tell you now that the first person must be you. If you don't support yourself, you will find it hard to see that other people are also on your side. It should be easy but it's often difficult and a lot of distress is caused when we don't act as our best supporter.

This is about having compassion for yourself. Without it you'll blame yourself for everything, you will fail to see the strengths you have and you'll be far harsher on yourself than others are being and harsher than you are on other people. If you're being bullied or abused, you'll think you deserve it; if you're struggling with schoolwork, you'll tell yourself it's because you're stupid; if your mental health is low, you'll label yourself as weak; if someone is mean to you, you'll believe it's because you're in some way unlikeable and you'll think that you have to change in order to be loved.

All those things will damage your resilience. You'll find it hard to move forward and bounce back from anything because you won't believe you can or that you deserve success, happiness or fulfilment.

If you saw a young animal being kicked, how would you feel about it? Would you think it must deserve to be kicked? That it was unworthy of love? No, you'd feel compassion for it. You'd believe that it deserved to be cared for and ought not to be abused.

Compassion is when you feel that you're on that creature's side. You might not know exactly how it feels but you have some connection with that feeling – some empathy – and most of all you wish you could take away the animal's pain because you know that even if it had behaved in an annoying way, it still didn't deserve to be kicked. You might also guess that the animal is being kicked because the *abuser* is angry or lacking in control or very stressed or has a problem with power. But you know that, whatever the reason, the animal should not be kicked. You're on that animal's side; you are its supporter: you feel compassion.

That young animal needs someone to feel compassion: it can't do it for itself. But you are a human and you *can* feel compassion for another creature, another human and for yourself.

You need first to feel compassion for yourself. You owe yourself that.

In practice, this means that when something bad happens:

♥ You don't blame yourself for other people's actions.

- ♥ You don't take the blame for things happening that are out of your control.
- ♥ You don't say to yourself, "These things happen to you because that's what you deserve."
- ♥ You treat yourself as you would treat another creature in distress.

Being compassionate to yourself doesn't mean turning a blind eye to any mistakes you made. If you did make a mistake, your voice of compassion should acknowledge that but show how you will try not to make the same mistake again.

Depending on the situation, think of what a friend or supporter would say; you just need to remember to say it to yourself. Here are some things your voice of compassion might say to you:

- ♥ "Sometimes things go wrong and it's nothing to do with you: it's bad luck or other people."
- ♥ "You're not responsible for the bad or cruel things other people do."
- ♥ "Everyone makes mistakes – good people learn from them. You can learn from this and I can help you."
- ♥ "I believe in you: you have strengths and you are valuable."

You are your own first supporter, the first person on your own team. Your job is to be kind and loyal to yourself and to believe in your value. Your job is also to be honest but to be honest with gentleness and compassion, looking to how you can become a better person, learn from your mistakes and grow.

PRACTICAL ACTIVITY

Think of something bad that happened to you. It could be when you had an argument with a friend, or someone was nasty to you or you did badly in a test. In your head play the role of someone who is completely on your side. What would they say to you? If this feels difficult, what would you say to someone you like who is having this experience and feeling really distressed about it? Would you criticise them? Would you tell them it's their fault and they just need to be a better person? No, you'd comfort them, reassure them, help them find ways to prevent the problem again, help them find ways to move forward and be strong. So, talk to yourself like that: be the voice of compassion in your own head.

Do this any time something negative has happened or is happening.

KNOW YOUR TEAM

Now that you know that you are your own first supporter, you need to know who the rest of your team are. This will be different for everyone. It's all about who you have some kind of bond with and there are more than you might think!

You have many of these bonds, though you might not have thought about it. You have bonds with your family, including any who don't live in the same house as you. Do you have grandparents or aunts and uncles? You might have very strong or less strong bonds with them, depending on how much contact you have (face to face or on video calls or whatever communication method) and how they interact with you. It's not about how much you love someone, which isn't really possible to measure and isn't helpful to judge. It's more about how well you feel you know them, how likely you would be to tell them your news or ask them a question.

Even if you don't feel very close to someone, you can have a bond with them. For example, supposing you have an aunt that you see once a year and you don't feel you know her very well at all. You still have a bond – she's connected to you by being related. She cares about what happens to you.

You probably have connections with other adults, too: anyone whose name you know and to whom you don't feel negatively. And there will be fellow students at school or other young people who live nearby who, even if you don't call yourselves friends, you do have some kind of connection with, some kind of reason to trust them. If you bumped into them on holiday or in a shop, you'd smile and you might say "Hi". Would they help you if you were hurt? If so, they count.

Let's look at your team of connections. Consider your own situation as you think about each one. Try to think about who would be on your side if you needed help. Some might be strongly and always on your side; with others, you might feel it depends on the situation.

- ❤ The adults who directly care for you and live with you at least part of the time: parents or other carers. You might have one or several adults who are strongly bonded to you. You might turn to different ones for different types of help.
- ❤ Other adults related to you: grandparents, aunts, uncles.
- ❤ Adults who are family friends – you might live near them or they might live far away, even overseas.
- ❤ Any siblings. You might have good relationships with them or less so, but it's likely they'd be happy to help if you had a problem or needed support.
- ❤ Your close friends at school and home – people you see often.

- Less-close friends — perhaps people in your class at school who you feel positively towards but you wouldn't say are your close friends. You'd be happy to be put with them to do a project and you'd chat a bit if you bumped into each other but you don't go to each other's house to hang out.
- People with whom you play sport, do drama or singing, take part in hobbies or play computer games.
- The adults who lead those activities — assuming they follow the same rules of safeguarding as school teachers do.
- Social workers, doctors, any medical professionals.
- Adults in your school: teachers, librarians, pastoral staff, school nurse or counsellor, your head of year.

If you write those names down, how does that list look? Bigger than you expected? That's wonderful, but it doesn't matter if it's not very long. A few trusted connections is all you need. At any one moment you may only need one or two people to turn to, but it's useful to have a few more because different people can help in different ways and in different situations.

You need to know who you can turn to for any of the following:

- To help if you have a worry, however strange you might feel it is.
- To be on your side if someone is treating you badly.
- To reassure you when you doubt your abilities.
- To have fun with.
- To relax with.
- To be honest but kind in their opinions.
- To give wise, caring advice.
- To help you solve a problem.

- ❤ To help you come up with good ideas.
- ❤ To discuss a big topic that people disagree about – to see what you think and test out your ideas and opinions.

You also need to know that someone will be thinking of you even if you don't ask for help. You need someone:

- ❤ To notice when you seem down.
- ❤ To ask if you need help but to give you space if you don't.
- ❤ To want to spend time with you.
- ❤ To worry about you.
- ❤ To care what happens to you.

We also need to consider individual strengths and weaknesses, which might mean we get support from a particular person on some matters but not others. For example, someone could be a good friend but perhaps they disagree with you on an aspect of politics or hold a different moral position from you on something: in that case you would not go to them for strong advice or ideas on those things. It's OK to feel safe talking to someone about one subject but not about another. It's OK to choose to go to different people for support in different circumstances.

I believe it helps our resilience if we have a range of different views and outlooks in our support network. That way we can hear the other side of arguments and understand that people have different views but can still be good people who are part of our life. I don't think we become more resilient by only listening to one viewpoint or knowing one type of person. Trees become stronger when they experience the wind blowing. If you only ever hear one viewpoint, you'll think that's all there is and you won't have a chance to test your beliefs and make them stronger or alter them if that seems the right thing to do.

Remember that resilience is not about preventing negative things: it's about making yourself strong for when they come. And the people around us are a big part of that – not to stop bad things happening to us (because they can't), but to help us when they do. Our support network is there to be like a protective shell, helping us avoid damage; it is not like a cave that we never leave.

PRACTICAL ACTIVITY

Make a mind map, with yourself in a circle at the middle. Nearby, write the names of the people you feel are your most trusted connections and put each one in a circle. Then, a bit further out from you, write the names of some of the other people you are connected to.

Next to each name, write something positive about your relationship or connection to them. For example, "I would trust him with a worry" or "She always seems to understand how I'm feeling". And also write down what type of problem you might ask them for help with or tell them about.

That's your team. There's something that connects them: you trust them. Let's look at what trust is and how you can build it.

ALL ABOUT TRUST

We need people we trust but we should not trust everyone we meet. Some people will treat us badly or won't care about our welfare. Some people have desires or priorities which conflict with our needs and those people may well put their needs before ours. That's understandable because we might put our needs above those of someone else: in fact, putting our needs high on our own list of priorities is important and right.

Some individuals trust too easily and some don't trust enough. Trusting is about feeling safe and knowing when we are safe and when we are not. We can't feel one hundred per cent safe all the time because life does and will always contain risk, but we do need to feel safe sometimes and to make correct judgements about when we are safe.

TRUSTING TOO EASILY

Trusting too easily can mean that we are tricked, conned or disappointed. And not just by people: we might be too trusting of media headlines, videos, advertisements and political messages. We might not spot the signs that someone is deceiving us. Here are some reasons why a person might trust too easily:

- ♥ They might have had a very sheltered upbringing, with masses of support and love and adults doing things for them, so they have never experienced someone behaving negatively towards them.

- ♥ They might have had a very difficult upbringing which means they are desperate to be loved and they might not be cautious enough when someone appears to like them.

- ♥ They might not have learnt some useful ways to decide whether what they read or hear is likely to be true.

NOT TRUSTING ENOUGH

Not trusting enough can mean that we never open up to people, which will make it harder to build new friendships. We might make it obvious we don't trust them, which is likely to drive them away. We might suspect people of being deceitful or unfaithful when they're not. We might believe *nothing* we read or hear, even things which are true and useful, so we miss opportunities.

Here are some reasons why a person might find it hard to trust:

- ♥ They might have been let down a lot – or have been let down very badly once and now be very affected by it.

- ♥ They might have had a very difficult early childhood, not building the necessary "attachment" with one or more caregivers. (Attachment theory, developed by psychologist John Bowlby in the 1970s, shows the importance of a baby feeling strongly cared for by one or two consistent loving adults who attend to all the baby's needs. Babies who don't receive this, for whatever reason – including many things which are not the parents' fault – can develop poor attachment, and one of the results of this can be problems with trust and relationships later.)

- ♥ They might have been brought up by adults who found it hard to trust and this attitude has rubbed off on them.

HOW TO TRUST WISELY

We shouldn't trust everyone but we must trust some people. So we need to learn how to make the best possible guesses about whom to trust. The good news is that if we find trust difficult, we can learn to trust more easily, and if we are too trusting we can learn to be wiser in our choices.

Here are some guidelines for trusting wisely when it comes to individuals who might be in your support network:

1. Tune into how you really feel about a person. When

you are with them, face to face, do you feel safe and comfortable? Body language and eye contact can tell us a lot, as long as we really try to be honest rather than just seeing what we want to see.

2. Check there's no reason to mistrust. If there is, what is it? Is it that someone has told you something negative about them? (If so, can you trust that information?) Is it because they've let you down before? (People can make mistakes and genuinely regret it and not do it again; but some people will keep on doing it and won't change. Be careful how many chances you give someone.)

3. If you feel any doubt, give the person a chance but be cautious what information you share. You can have friendships where you don't give away your inner thoughts.

4. With adults who are not relatives or friends of your family, think about whether they are in jobs where they will know the rules of safeguarding and how to respond appropriately to your needs: for example, teachers and medical professionals.

5. With other adults who are relatives or friends of your family, listen to how you really feel about the person: the chances are your instincts are right. (But instincts are not one hundred per cent reliable.)

WHO IS A TRUSTED ADULT?

You'll often read advice, including from me, that suggests that you talk to a trusted adult. Sometimes, it's obvious who your trusted adults are. But what if it's not obvious? And is it possible to be wrong and have your trust betrayed?

What I *don't* mean is someone who will always keep your secrets or someone who will always have the right answer.

Sometimes adults need to share something you've told them in confidence because it's the right thing to do: to protect you, for example. They should usually discuss this with you, though. Sometimes, also, adults don't know the answers. Sometimes, adults may have big problems of their own, which might affect their ability to help you.

What I mean by a trusted adult is someone who genuinely tries to do the right thing and help you; someone who is on your side. Someone who will worry about you and care.

Let's look at who these people might be. And then I'll give you some guidelines to follow in those cases where you are not completely sure this person is a trusted adult.

- ❤ **Related adults** – I hope the adults in your family – your parents or carers, grandparents, aunts and uncles – are all trusted adults. They should be but sometimes they aren't. With these people, it's right to start by assuming that they are unless you have a good reason to think that they aren't. (See "When you might not trust", on page 44.) These are people who are connected to you and *should* have your interests at heart.

- ❤ **Adults in professional settings** – These include teachers and other adults working in your school; doctors and other medical professionals; and social workers. Nowadays, all adults who work regularly with young people have to have two safeguards which are designed to keep you safe: training in appropriate behaviour with young people and training in how to react if a young person comes to them with a problem. They qualify as a trusted adult. However, these safeguards are not one hundred per cent secure and it is possible for a potentially dangerous person to be in one of these settings. It's unlikely in a school, but it does happen. Don't ignore your instincts about this.

- ♥ **Other adults you meet** – This could be any adult who interacts with you in any setting at all. Most adults who seem to want to help you *do* want to help you, but you know that bad individuals can also trick you into trusting them. Therefore, you should be very careful.

- ♥ **Anyone you "meet" only online** – This is the best-known setting where adults with bad intentions can trick you into trusting them. You don't have your visual instincts and body language to help you judge. Also, as you very well know, people can lie about their age online. The only way to be completely sure that it's OK to trust an adult you're engaging with online is if you are doing so through a recognised organisation such as Childline or a mental health charity. If not, tell another known and trusted adult if you connect with someone online, so they can help you be safe.

WHEN YOU MIGHT NOT TRUST

It's not always obvious whether someone can be trusted but there are some considerations which will help you decide:

1. The relationship or friendship you have with the person should not be secret or hidden: if you feel you have to hide it from your other trusted adults, this is a danger sign.

2. If they ask you to keep a secret, this is a negative sign. Why are they burdening you with this? If they ask you to keep a secret from your parents or carers, this is a very bad sign. (Unless it's something fun, such as a birthday present or nice surprise.)

3. Does the person make you feel uncomfortable? Is there something they're doing that you don't like – for example, touching you or sitting too close? Talk to another adult if you're not sure about your instincts.

4. Listen to your instincts. If you are worried about anything at all, don't consider this person a trusted adult. Trust is yours to give and theirs to earn.

PRACTICAL ACTIVITY

Write down one or more people you would or could talk to about any of these situations:

Schoolwork worries; being bullied; a relationship worry; a medical worry that felt embarrassing to talk about; hating your appearance; feeling like an outsider or different from others; problems with a teacher; a worry about one or more of your parents; questions about sex; if someone you knew was taking drugs; if you thought someone was behaving really badly/criminally and you didn't know what to do; a worry about your future; major emotions that you couldn't control; harming yourself or thinking about it; if you were thinking about suicide.

Feel grateful that you have those people to turn to. If there are gaps in your list, think whether there's a teacher or other professional or an online organisation that you could use to get good information. Information can support you, too.

Important note: if you ever think about harming yourself or taking your life or about how you would do it, please get help without delay. You can call one of the helplines at the back of this book, for free expert and confidential help.

Even if we follow all the guidelines, we might sometimes make a mistake. If you make a wrong judgement, positive or negative, about another person, this does not mean you are a bad judge of people. Instead, each time you make such a mistake, try to learn from it and add it to your understanding of human beings. Everything you learn builds your resilience for future decisions and situations.

BUILDING GOOD FRIENDSHIPS

On page 37 you saw a list of things we might need from the people we're connected to. And you've thought about people you know who might tick at least some of those boxes, some of whom are your friends. If you're lucky, those friendships are going well, but what if they're not?

Here are a few tips for building and strengthening good friendships. The same tips apply as you go through life and make new friends, as you certainly will.

- ♥ **Appreciate people's differences** – Not all your friends (or others in your support network) are identical to you in needs or wants. Notice when you have a friend whose needs differ from yours: for example, perhaps they need excitement and noise while you require peace and quiet. You can still be friends if you accommodate each other's differences.

- ♥ **Be a good listener** – When a friend wants to talk, listen attentively. You don't have to have an answer, but listen carefully and try to understand what they feel. Try not to dismiss their worries as silly but accept that what they say they feel *is* what they feel.

- ♥ **Give and take** – In a good friendship, each person gives and receives, but not necessarily at the same time. Sometimes you might need to give support and at others you might need to receive it. There will be times when one person needs more support and that's fine. It's good to be generous but it can become a problem if it's very one-sided all the time. Supposing you are giving masses of support to a friend in need but you find you need support yourself: you might need to get that support from a different person.

- **Spend time on the friendship** – All relationships, but some more than others, need some effort. This is why we can't really manage too many friends. (The number of "friends" some people have on social media far exceeds the number they can truly spend time on. You might like to know that the evolutionary biologist, Robin Dunbar, has said that 150 is approximately the maximum number – "Dunbar's number". There's a reference to his work in the Resources section, page 187.) Spending time on a friendship could involve talking, playing a game, hanging out, asking how your friend is, cheering them up or just being there in some way.

- **Create positive memories of times shared with your friends** – It's fun to look back on happy times and say to a friend "Remember when we…" These memories can also help us get through difficult times in our relationships. Find shared experiences you can have, whether it's a trip, cinema visit, ice cream in a café, picnic or expedition. Take photos and keep mementoes!

- **Be true to yourself** – Sometimes people find themselves in friendships with people they don't *really* like or identify with. Perhaps you feel you don't have a choice; or you were flattered by a popular person's attention; or you joined a group for your own security; or you started off liking these people but you're discovering that now you don't. You do not have to be friends with people you're not comfortable with and in fact you could do yourself a favour (and show compassion to yourself) by walking away from this situation. This does not mean you have to agree with your friends on everything! You'll find more advice on this in the rest of this chapter.

PRACTICAL ACTIVITY

Can you think of a friend – whether close or more distant, old or new – who has recently stepped up and helped you in some way? If so, have you thanked them properly? Or do you know someone who has been going through a hard time recently? If so, could you send them a message or do something to show you care about them? Gifts are obviously lovely things but an act of giving doesn't have to cost anything: it could be a hand-made note, a text or email, a photo to remind them of a fun time, a flower picked from the garden, a painted pebble or a shell from a beach, a hug – even just a few words to show that you appreciate what they did or that they are your friend.

DEALING WITH NEGATIVE CONNECTIONS

There might be people around you who have a negative impact. This could be anyone that you come across either at home, at school, in your neighbourhood or online. They could be former friends, siblings or stepfamily members, teachers you can't get on with, people who just seem not to like you.

They may be people who, for one reason or another, make you feel bad, fearful, insecure and unable to do your best. They could be your age, or any age. They might or might not be doing it deliberately. It might just be that you're both very different from each other, or any reason why there's none of the chemistry that positive bonds need.

Although it's not always possible to avoid such connections, here are some ideas that might apply to certain situations:

♥ You don't have to continue with a broken or damaged friendship. It's tough when a friendship ends but it is common and natural as we all change through our lives. Try to put it in context, to accept that this has happened and that you will make new friends. Try to avoid blame (even in your head), whether of yourself or the other person. Move on and leave it behind, acknowledging anything you learnt and gained from it.

♥ You do not have to tolerate abuse, whether emotional or physical. If you can, walk away from the situation; if you need help, ask a trusted adult. Every situation is different so it would be wrong of me to give specific advice here, but teachers and other professionals working with young people can offer the right support. If you can't speak to them, contact a national charity or organisation dedicated to helping young people (such as Childline in the UK).

♥ Someone who often makes you feel bad about yourself is not a good supporter. A friend might offer genuinely constructive criticism, which can be useful even if not exactly pleasant. (No one enjoys criticism but sometimes we need it!) This is different from constant undermining, which is not the mark of a good friend. Perhaps you can ask them why they do this; or you might prefer to walk away and let the friendship fade. They might not be able to help it but someone who makes you feel bad about yourself is not part of your support network.

♥ If your negative connection is someone in your own home, you might need a trusted adult to help you through this. Siblings and step-siblings often have rocky relationships or phases, perhaps with personality clashes, rivalry and competing need for affection and attention. It may be no one's fault but a wise person can help you see a way through it.

♥ What if the problem is with one of the adults who care for you? This is such a varied situation that the best advice is to speak to another trusted adult, who might be able to show you a different way of looking at things or to find a strategy to improve the situation. It's quite common to feel that your parents or carers are against you because conflict often arises between teenagers and adults and sometimes emotions (on either side) get in the way of reason. But it's also fair to say that some parents don't or can't give the support that's needed. In that case, asking another adult for help is a useful starting point.

Some might argue that dealing with negative connections will surely make us stronger and more resilient. Should we not just accept that not everyone will be on our side? Certainly, we need to be realistic and recognise that not everyone *is* on our side. But I'm emphasising the need to focus on building up our *good* relationships because that support network will be part of our toolkit for tough times, helping us grow the resilience that we will need as we go through life. Yes, we need to deal with negative people but we don't need to welcome them into our lives and let them weaken us!

BEING RESILIENT TO DISAGREEMENT

This leads on to something which has become ever more important in today's often hostile environment, especially online: dealing with strong disagreement and opposing views. The arguments on social media and in the media in general are often extreme, with people taking completely polarised positions and being aggressive and even threatening to people who think differently from them. Then it often becomes one person's support network fighting another and it's usually really painful and distressing for the people involved.

But it should be possible to disagree – even disagree strongly – without shouting at each other or being insulting. We need to learn how to explain our viewpoints and to listen to others. Here are some things to consider:

- ♥ On most subjects, there are different viewpoints which intelligent and decent people could hold, depending on things such as their experiences, their view of the world, their likes and dislikes, their politics and what matters to them most. (It's OK for us to differ on all those things.) Some viewpoints are easier to defend than others; some *are* based on hatred or anger or intolerance, but others are based on different interpretations of the world we live in and different important experiences people have had.

- ♥ It's better to criticise someone's views and ideas rather than them as a person. (Criticising someone personally – their character or appearance, for example – is called an "ad hominem" attack, which just means "against the person".) Once there are personal comments and attacks, the actual argument is usually lost in the aggression and noise.

- ♥ Listening to the reasons behind a differing viewpoint is usually useful and revealing. I'm not suggesting you listen to the "reasons" behind hateful words, as hateful words come from emotions, more than reasons. But when someone is arguing a different viewpoint from yours it can help you strengthen your own viewpoint if you understand *why* they think as they do. Often, if you listen properly, you find they aren't actually saying what you first thought they were. Listening to their ideas can help you test your own reasoning, too.

- ♥ If someone says something cruel or abusive to you and you feel hurt, your feelings matter and are valid. This is when your support network can be most helpful, allowing you to find ways to respond, which might include walking away or calling the person out on their behaviour. The appropriate response depends on the situation and different people will have different views about how to deal with it. This is the time to breathe and think and listen to trusted friends.

♥ Social media is almost always a bad place to have an argument or discussion on serious matters! People keep getting involved when they haven't heard the beginning of it; they jump to conclusions; and they feel emboldened to be much ruder and more thoughtless than they would be face to face. In fact, there's a name for this: "online disinhibition effect", describing the fact that most people are less careful, thoughtful and controlled when interacting online, rather than face to face or on a phone call.

♥ It is OK and normal to have friends with whom you don't agree on everything. Sometimes you can "agree to disagree" on a particular topic and keep it out of the conversation. Obviously, if the point you disagree on is something really fundamental to you then this might not be possible and it is your right to walk away from the relationship. But if you only have friends who agree with you on everything, you'll have a narrow outlook.

It will help if you can build resilience to disagreement because it will enable you not to take it personally when someone you respect takes a different view from you. It will help you keep such moments or situations in perspective and not let them drag you down. You will be able to engage with the disagreement (if you wish to) in a strong and reasoned way or to walk away and leave it behind if you prefer to do that. And your own arguments will be stronger if they come from reason rather than an emotional response of upset, stress or anger.

However, when someone does upset you by making ad hominem remarks or by taking a view that you fundamentally disagree with or feel offended by, you are allowed to be offended and to say so. That's not a lack of resilience. Resilience is about strength – the strength to respond in any way you feel is right (including walking away or staying silent), and not to be dragged down or made to feel weaker. These are the times when you most need your good, honest, wise friends who care about you and to listen to their advice.

The best support network is one that is diverse, so that you see many points of view and experiences, which will help keep you strong, knowledgeable, flexible and wise. It is made up of people who know you, understand you and care about you. When they disagree they will do so respectfully.

ASK FOR HELP WHEN YOU NEED IT

Now that you have identified your support network (beginning with yourself), how are they going to help your resilience? Simply knowing that they're there, on your side, is a very good start. Knowing that you have people who care about you and who would respond if you needed them goes a long way to giving you mental strength.

But you have to be able to ask for their help. When you need to do this, here are some tips:

- ♥ **Choose the right person** – You'll probably have a sense of who can help you best in different situations. You'll turn to different people for problems with schoolwork, friendships, anxiety about exams or anxiety about an illness or family situation. Look back at the activity you did on page 45.
- ♥ **Choose the right moment** – Asking someone for help when they are too busy, or very stressed or worrying about

someone else, may make it hard for them to listen properly and respond. It is often a good idea to tell them you'd like to talk to them and then let them choose when.

- ♥ **Choose the right medium** – The way you choose to have a conversation makes a difference; as well as face to face, there's email, text, private messaging, written note or phone. Each of these has advantages and disadvantages. Face to face is good for checking understanding but can be scary; texting or messaging is quite informal and simple but can make it difficult to convey exact meanings in emotional situations; a written note can be very powerful and meaningful but can sometimes seem too "heavy" and formal.

- ♥ **Choose the right place** – When a topic is difficult to talk about or you feel anxious about it, discussing it while walking or while in a car can help. This is because you don't have to make eye contact and you also don't have to fill every moment with words.

- ♥ **Choose the right opening** – You might need to warn someone that you're about to say something really important. "I have a problem I need your help with" alerts them to pay attention and take you seriously.

- ♥ **Choose the right words** – It can be really difficult to find the right words but it's OK to say "This is really difficult to explain", or that you have something to say which is awkward or tricky. Framing the conversation in this way, so that the person starts listening to you with extra patience, is a good idea.

- ♥ **Choose the right aim** – Are you expecting the person to listen and empathise, or to advise, or to give an opinion? Or do you just need information? Being realistic about what the other person can do is important. Often, just having someone to share your emotions or thoughts with is all you need.

♥ **Think about whether you are sharing confidential information** – You will need to say that it's confidential but be aware that keeping secrets can be difficult and sometimes impossible. For example, the person might need to tell someone if they think you (or someone else) are in danger.

Remember that people usually do want to help and, if you've gathered the right supporters, they certainly will.

Remember, too, that people like to be appreciated, even if they gave their help completely happily. So, when anyone has been supportive to you in any way, big or small, it is great to acknowledge that and thank them as soon as you can.

GIVE HELP TO OTHERS WHEN THEY NEED IT

You know the phrase "You scratch my back and I'll scratch yours"? When you see chimpanzees or other apes sitting and picking fleas out of each other's fur, they're not just doing it as a favour: it's how they bond socially. It's useful because it keeps the whole group clean and healthy but it also creates bonds, connections that link them so that they will help each other in other ways, too.

Social bonds, friendships and work connections are a two-way process: you help me and I'll help you. We don't *say* that and we don't usually consciously *think* it but it's how friendships and partnerships work: we help each other, rather than just expecting others to help us. Of course, we do care about people who can't help us: babies, for example, or people who are sick or unable to look after themselves in some way. We don't do it so that they will help us back, but giving to others makes it more likely that we will be helped when we need it, by others in our community.

As I write this, we are living through the COVID-19 lockdown and in good communities friends and neighbours are doing a lot for each other. We all have different skills, opportunities, strengths and needs. Some people have to shield carefully because of underlying health conditions so they need others to do shopping and errands for them; they show their gratitude in words and gestures. No one is keeping a list of who has done what and who is doing more but it's obvious that everyone is doing what they can, when they can. If there was someone who *couldn't* help or give, we'd support them willingly; but if someone who *could* help and *could* give never did or never showed they were grateful, people might start to be resentful and might choose to spend their time on others. The bonds that connect us would become weaker and might break.

That's the unspoken contract between humans: we help each other and the feeling of connection has to go both ways. We don't keep score but we sense when someone never tries to play their part.

What about families? This is a little bit different from connections with people who are not related to you in any way. Your parents, grandparents and aunts and uncles are all likely to be on your side and be strong supporters of you even if you don't do anything in return. However, it is a great idea to help them when you can, too! It might strengthen the bonds and make it easier for them to devote time to you when you need it. And it will make you feel good, too.

Often, just keeping in touch with messages, texts or little cards is enough. Write a thank you note or ask someone how they are. It can make a big difference.

REBUILD YOUR NETWORK AFTER A BAD TIME

All this advice has been about building your support network to give you resilience before and during a difficult time, but what about *after* a bad thing has happened? Supposing you've just had a time when you couldn't have fun with your friends because you were suffering anxiety, or bad news, exam stress, worry at home or some kind of relationship breakdown. You probably relied on some of your support network during that time and it's possible some of those connections were strained. Maybe one even broke irreparably. Or perhaps you felt that you didn't have the support you needed or you didn't make the best use of what you had? How are you going to build up your resilience again for the future? Here is some advice.

1. Think about how the people in your support network *did* help you. Think about and acknowledge to yourself how important it felt that there was someone you could connect with and who was there for you, or who would have been if you'd asked.

2. If there's anyone who you need to thank or praise or acknowledge for their help, do so as soon as you can.

3. If any friendship has been broken and you don't want to or can't repair it, try to let this go and move on, focusing instead on your positive connections. If you do that, everything else will work itself out or fade into the background.

4. Find ways to have fun with friends and family, with anyone you feel positive towards and whose relationship you value. These enjoyable moments and experiences will build the bonds between you all, create happy memories to look back on *and* help grow a positive outlook. All those will play their part in strengthening your resilience for the future.

REFLECTION ACTIVITY

Go back to page 24 and reread about Abbie, Chris and Seema. Think about what their support networks might be and whether they can use them better or make them stronger so that they can be more resilient in future difficult situations.

What do you think Abbie's problems are? What could she do about them? Is she making some mistakes in her thinking? Have you got some suggestions for her? Who might she talk to? Do you think she should talk to Bilal about how she feels?

What do you think about how Bilal and Abbie stopped being friends? Is there anything they might have done differently?

What are Chris's main problems? Who could be his support network? Who could he talk to? If you were Chris's friend, what would you say to him? What should he do about his brother? Do you think Chris will be OK?

Seema needs someone to step in and help her because she's not well and not seeing things straight. Who should help Seema get the treatment she needs? Do you think her friends are really jealous? What do you think her friends should do to help her? Does she have a good support network?

Is there someone you know who is going through similar challenges to any of them? Or perhaps even yourself? How would you advise them?

On page 176, you'll find my personal answers to those questions.

SUMMING UP

Your support network is a very valuable way to keep you strong for the future and to support you through tough times; recognising and appreciating it will help make you resilient. Most of the time, we don't have to do anything very deliberate or special to grow our groups of friends and contacts: we just have to follow our instincts to communicate and spend time with people we like and trust. Even those of us who like to spend time alone sometimes want to be with or chat to another person, and it makes sense to do that when we feel like it.

But sometimes we need to make a special effort and be social when we're not feeling like it or when our circumstances make it more challenging. On those occasions, it's worth thinking about who our real friends and supporters are, so that we can find ways to stay connected with them and to strengthen the bonds that make humans work and play together.

Remember that you don't have to agree with your friends or family on everything but it's most likely that you'll be firmest friends with people who mostly share your values and beliefs. Your best resilience will come when you talk and listen to people who care about you, so you can grow strong and face storms in partnership, like trees bending and swaying and maturing together.

TOP TIPS FOR BUILDING YOUR SUPPORT NETWORK

1. Don't count your friends: the number doesn't matter. But do think about who you can count on and make sure they can count on you.

2. Good friendships take time and effort. Spare time for your friends, to listen to them or hang out with them; when you can't – when you are too overwhelmed yourself, for

example – look for the next chance.

3. Use these words whenever you think it would be helpful: "please", "thank you", "sorry", "well done" and "I'm here for you". Use them with yourself, too, because you have to be your own voice of support.

4. Be a listener more than a talker.

5. When you have the chance to meet new people – or get to know existing acquaintances better – take it. You never know what might come from it.

DIARY TIME

You can write anything in your diary, of course, including all the practical activities, but here are some ideas:

1. Three things you learnt from this chapter.

2. Make a list of the people who you feel are on your side and would help if you asked them and if they could. Include people your age and adults, if possible.

3. Did you identify or empathise with any of the imaginary characters from the start of this chapter?

4. Is there something you will try to do differently after reading this chapter?

5. Has a friend helped you or been kind to you recently? Write about this.

6. Write a short letter of support to yourself.

CHAPTER THREE

BUILD YOUR SKILLS

HOW DOES THIS HELP RESILIENCE?

Building skills is an important part of building resilience in two ways: first, when you see that you can learn and improve anything by practising, you can apply that knowledge to help you bounce back after something you've found very difficult or when you feel you've failed. Second, building skills of any sort grows your confidence in general and confidence is a big part of resilience.

I could have called this chapter "Build your confidence", but confidence comes from first building skills and recognising them. Develop skills and you'll boost your resilience. Some people call this "mastery": being able to do something. You can have mastery of a topic when you know lots about it; or you can have mastery of a skill when you have practised it enough that you can do it easily.

TEENAGE EXAMPLES

These characters are all in the same class at school and are just starting to learn French. They've had a couple of lessons and the teacher is about to test what they've learnt so far by asking them to answer some questions and read aloud. How resilient will they be to doing badly or struggling in the test? How they react to one small setback might well reflect how they react to bigger ones, too.

♥ ♥ ♥

Eddie lives with his mum and her new partner, who are always encouraging and praising him. He loves that, of course – who wouldn't? He's the oldest of three siblings and he's used to doing everything first and better than his younger brother and sister. That makes him feel good about himself. At primary school, Eddie was always being praised. His mum would always tell him all the things he was good at. Trouble is, the work this year is harder and his friend Fardin has been doing better than him quite often. Eddie is sure he saw disappointment in his mum's eyes when Fardin won a prize and Eddie didn't. So maybe he's losing his skills? Maybe he's no good after all?

♥ ♥ ♥

Fardin and Sadia are twins but they are very different. Sadia is confident and doesn't seem to mind whether she does well or not; she's quite happy to try something and fail or find it hard. She'll just shrug it off and try again; sometimes she even laughs at her own mistakes. Actually, that's all a bit of a front: she is doing it as a defence mechanism and inside she thinks she's useless at everything except making people laugh. Her parents tell her not to be such a clown but that doesn't stop her, it just reinforces that that's what she is.

Fardin absolutely hates it when he can't do something really well first time – he feels self-conscious, embarrassed and useless. He's been told he's bright all his life and is doing really well at school, but it's never good enough (for him) unless he's top of the class. He is good friends with Eddie but they've been falling out lately because Eddie gets cross when Fardin does better than him. Fardin's parents tell him, "You're a clever boy, Fardin, but maybe it would be better if you did some different things from Eddie. You might find you're good at something else."

Mattie is dyslexic, like her dad. This means that there are some things she struggles with – particularly when they involve reading aloud or writing. This used to make her really upset when she saw her friends finding it easy to read and spell. But she has developed a strong memory for things she's heard. Her dad encourages this and together they spend time learning lists of facts, such as capital cities or the dates of American presidents. And in the last year she's had a great learning support teacher who shows her ways of improving the things she finds hard. She has her reading age measured every now and then and it's clear she's making good progress. Sometimes she feels awful when she has to read aloud but people have stopped teasing her about it now.

••••

The teacher knows these students well but she doesn't know what's going on inside their minds. Their ways of thinking have been partly formed by all their different life experiences and family situations and personalities, so she doesn't know the effect that this lesson will have.

The lesson begins. And it's much harder than all of them expected! Eddie's mind goes blank when it's his turn and he stumbles over a simple word. He feels himself go red and the teacher asks someone else to take over, which makes him feel a failure, even though he's glad not to be in the limelight any more. Sadia also makes a mistake and laughs at herself, although she's cursing herself inside. Messed up again, Sadia! Fardin knows he's not going to be able to get it right so just blurts out the quickest answer he can and doesn't hear what the teacher says. Mattie does really well because she's memorised the answer, which was actually the perfect set of skills to use for this exercise. But instead of feeling good about it, she's thinking, Thank goodness I didn't have to write it down – if I had, I'd have failed. Then she makes a mental note to get her dad or her learning support teacher to help her practise writing it, before thinking, No, hang on – I could do that myself. All I have to do is practise properly and I know how to do that.

All those students thought the test was difficult. All of them lost confidence in themselves, though Mattie got it back again. The others didn't recognise the skills they'd used or enjoy the challenge; only Mattie remembered that learning requires determination and is a journey which begins with one step and proceeds one step at a time. She knows she's built a good memory and she used it.

Mattie showed resilience in two quite different ways: first, she bounced back from the initial feelings of difficulty and failure and was able to keep learning and trying; second, she continued to build various abilities and skills, which made her feel good about herself and equipped her to succeed.

All of the characters could help themselves move forward and become stronger people. If they could become more like Mattie – both by understanding that they will improve anything by practising and by acquiring as many skills and abilities as possible – they could build brains that are more resilient to negative things that might happen to them. Their self-esteem has depended on other people's opinion of them and, unfortunately, some of the adults in their lives have accidentally helped create that situation. What they need is for their self-confidence to be stronger, so that they can treat any setback as an opportunity to do better next time, which they can only do if they believe in their potential. If they believe they can't do things, they won't want to try. If they believe that they can become better at something, they'll be empowered to try. They will become resilient to any experiences of failure because they will believe they can learn to succeed.

If you relate to any of those feelings and thoughts, it's time to look at your skills and your opinion of them. It's time to look at your confidence – the confidence you need in yourself, which Mattie showed despite the fact that she has a learning difficulty. Confidence in your ability to succeed will help make you resilient when things seem difficult. That applies both to relatively minor hurdles, like tests, as well as much bigger challenges you will face.

CONFIDENCE, SELF–ESTEEM AND PRAISE

I talked on page 18 about the difference between confidence and self-esteem, so you know that, although they are very similar, the more valuable one is confidence. This chapter is a very important one for building both confidence and self-esteem in order to become more resilient to challenges and setbacks. Confidence and real self-esteem come from building skills, much more than from being praised.

The problem is that too many people think that the way to boost someone's self-esteem or confidence is to keep praising them, telling them they're good at things, reassuring them that they can be anything they want to be, do anything they want, succeed in any way they choose. All those "inspirational" messages such as "You can do anything if you dream big enough" sound fine on the face of it. Encouraging and empowering, you would think.

Not necessarily. There are several reasons why these messages so often don't work and can sometimes even have the opposite effect:

♥ Very often such messages come from our parents or supportive teachers and we might not fully believe them because we think, Well, they would say that. They're just saying it to make me feel good.

- ♥ Such messages often come when we actually haven't done particularly well. Especially when we're young, we are often told we've done really well when in fact we can see with our own eyes that we haven't. Children are not that easily deceived! Yes, it's lovely to be reassured but, if we are praised when we don't do well, this can teach us not to trust the praise when we really do well.

- ♥ It is obviously untrue that you can be anything you want or achieve any target you set, just by trying. When we hear that message, we know in our hearts that it's not true. And each time it doesn't come true reinforces our distrust.

- ♥ We might get the message that all we have to do is try and we'll achieve what we want but that's not true either. There's a lot more to success than that: there's teaching, learning the right skills or information, listening, practising effectively – and luck.

When self-esteem is built from people praising us whatever we do, rather than when we have done well or worked hard, it's not very helpful, although it might feel nice at the time. If people want to praise constructively, in a way that will really help self-esteem, they need to praise for something we did actually do well. Maybe we prepared carefully, or tried hard, or kept going even though it was difficult, or overcame our nerves. If so, people should praise *those* things, rather than saying, "You did really well."

Of course, when someone is just beginning to learn something, they aren't expected to succeed as well as someone who has been learning for a while. So, a beginner needs praise even though they aren't doing something as well as someone more expert. "That was brilliant" for a novice pianist is different from "That was brilliant" for a practised player. But it needs to be genuine and true in each case, or the person won't feel that it was deserved. We need to *feel* that praise is deserved, otherwise it doesn't raise our self-esteem.

What we need in order to build our confidence and self-esteem are *skills*: mastery of the subjects or information or techniques which, when we've mastered them, *will* give us self-esteem. This will be self-esteem that comes from within us, rather than from other people. Then, when someone says, "You did a great job", you know you *did* do a great job: you listened carefully, worked hard, practised diligently, acted bravely. You made it happen yourself.

Being good at something is what gives confidence and pride, much more than being *told* you're great. And confidence is what is going to help you be resilient: confidence that you can survive and thrive.

So, this chapter is about building lots of skills, so that you can genuinely feel good about yourself and not rely on other people to say "well done". By having more confidence in your strengths, you will have better resilience when things seem difficult.

GROW A GROWTH MINDSET

You have probably heard of growth mindset, as it's something most teachers nowadays are keen to encourage in their students. "Mindset" means "an underlying way of thinking", and the phrase "growth mindset" was coined by the psychologist Carol Dweck, along with the phrase "fixed mindset".

Briefly, the difference is this:

If you have a **growth mindset** you tend to believe that when people are good at something it's because they have grown their skills through things such as good teaching, hard work and practice, and determination.

If you have a **fixed mindset** you tend to believe that when people are good at something it's mostly down to luck, talents that they were born with, inherited through their genes, for example.

Many people *say* they agree with the growth mindset approach, because we've all experienced becoming better at something when we learn and practise. But we've also probably all experienced finding something difficult and feeling that it just isn't something we can be good at. You can probably list things you're "good at" and things you're "bad at", and you may feel that trying to improve certain "weaknesses" will be a waste of time.

Many of us are somewhere between a growth mindset and a fixed one but the best way forward is to try to have as much of a growth mindset as possible. When a thought such as "I can't do this" comes along, we need to replace it with: "I find this difficult at the moment but there are steps I could take to gain better mastery. I just need to find those ways and practise well."

A growth mindset will improve your resilience, because when a failure happens you'll believe that you could succeed eventually; when a challenge comes that seems too difficult, you'll know you can find ways to become strong enough to overcome it; when anything goes wrong, you'll have the mindset to know that you can become stronger, with determination.

In fact, determination is very close to resilience itself.

Here are some ways to build a stronger growth mindset.

UNDERSTAND HOW THE BRAIN LEARNS

Every human baby is born with somewhere between 85 billion and 100 billion brain cells called neurons. That's around the same number as you have now. The main reason why a newborn baby can hardly do anything and has no deliberate skills but you can do loads of things really well, is that the baby's neurons are not connected up. You have built up billions of connections, enabling you to do a huge number of things you couldn't do when you were a baby.

These connections develop when you do these things:

- ❤ **Practise and try** – Every time you try to do something and do it again, new connections grow or old ones become stronger. When this happens, you become better at doing whatever it is.

- ❤ **Watch other people** – When we watch someone do something, some of the same neurons that we will use when we try the thing ourselves become active; so, when we do try, the connections have already started to form.

- ❤ **Take breaks** – When we've been trying to do something and then we take a break, the connections continue to develop. Some research suggests that taking physical exercise to break up mental activity is particularly useful for this.

- ❤ **Sleep** – Yes, connections grow while we sleep! When we've been working or trying really hard during the day, even struggling with something, our sleeping brain goes over those actions and helps grow and tidy up the connections.

Understanding this means that when you feel a bit negative about your ability to do something, you can remind yourself that the brain learns gradually, by practising, so your efforts will make you better. Then, when you struggle or make mistakes, you'll be resilient to those struggles and failures because you'll believe that you can improve.

SET GOALS THAT ARE REALISTIC AND OPTIMISTIC

If you set yourself goals that are too difficult, this can be a problem. It's important to find a balance between aiming too high and aiming too low. Your goals need to be not so high that they are impossible, but high enough that you can feel pleased when you achieve them: so, realistic but also optimistic, remembering that you can improve if you take the right steps.

Goals should always be:

♥ Specific, rather than vague.

♥ Measurable, so you can tell when you've achieved them.

♥ Realistic, rather than impossible.

A goal that fits these guidelines would be: "I will practise piano for 40 minutes five times a week." An unwise goal would be: "I will practise piano more" (too vague and hard to measure) or "I will practise for two hours a day every day" (unrealistic for most people!).

Some goals are immediate, such as "I will do an hour of practice before tea". Others are much more long-term, such as "I will pass my Grade 7 piano before I leave school".

Long-term goals need to be broken into smaller steps. If you have only just passed Grade 1 and you have to wait until you pass your Grade 7 before you can feel successful, you might feel demoralised early on. So, add in earlier targets of when you'll pass Grade 2 or 4 or whatever, and then work out what you need to do to get to them. Each good practice session is a step on the way to your short-term goal and that is a step towards your long-term goal.

Sometimes long-term goals seem very daunting. But remember that every journey of a thousand miles starts with one step. Gradually you can become better at the things you want to achieve, as long as you keep working hard and taking the right steps. You can't become a brilliant basketball player or writer or musician after two weeks, but you can become a better one than you are now.

You don't *have* to have clear long-term goals. It's perfectly OK to focus on the next few days or weeks. And certainly, when things are very tough for you, focusing on short-term aims is a really important strategy to keep your feet on the ground but moving in the right direction. However, in Chapter Six I will talk a bit more about how you can build your resilience with the help of some sensible longer-term goals.

It's also important to realise that you can't be good at everything. No one is. Yes, I know that there are people who *seem* to be good at everything – and it can be quite demoralising if we spend a lot of time with such people – but you're not seeing the whole picture. You see them achieve in schoolwork and sport, for example, but you don't see the things they aren't good at.

Why can't we be good at everything, if all it takes is practice and hard work? Because no one has enough hours in the day to practise everything and work hard on everything! It's healthy for us to enjoy a wide variety of activities, as you'll learn on page 79, but the aim is not to be brilliant at all of them, as that simply isn't possible. So, don't beat yourself up about the things you struggle with. (But do think about the next point...)

BE BRAVE – RISK FAILURE

A fixed mindset can make people only try things they believe they'll succeed at. "I'm not good at art so I won't try drawing a picture because it will be rubbish." Being "good at art" comes with practice and no one is good at it the first time they try. Every artist has spent hundreds – even thousands – of hours doing art, in other words *practising*. Same with anything: singing, cooking, building, speaking a foreign language. You have to start somewhere and that involves trying something even though you won't be good at it straightaway. It means accepting what will *feel* like failure for a while.

But it isn't failure! It's learning. It's just not *yet* being expert. Resilience comes when we accept that, with the right attitude, "failure" can lead to success.

Confidence isn't useful if it means you only do things you're *confident* you'll be good at. That's just safety, complacency. Truly useful confidence is when you trust yourself to try something and to deal with – and learn from – whatever the result is. Confidence is believing that you have the *potential* to be able to succeed, not the total belief that you will definitely succeed this time.

So, take risks with your learning. Try things that you're *not sure* you'll succeed in straightaway but which you believe you could; things you believe will benefit you. Have faith in your ability to try things and learn from them. That's resilience.

RECOGNISE HOW MUCH YOU'VE LEARNT

When we are finding life difficult for whatever reason, it's easy to feel that everything is too hard, that we'll never manage to overcome our challenges, that everyone is doing better than us.

If that's how you're feeling or how you feel sometimes, take a few minutes to think about and acknowledge how much you've learnt in your life. And then think about how young you are and how you know more than adults about some things. Look at small children trying to do something and see how much more you can do than them. You *learnt* those skills.

Value your character strengths just as much as any actual skills and knowledge you've acquired. Character strengths are skills of a sort but they are different from being able to read, write, do maths, play sport or musical instruments, sing, knit or make and bake. They are things like determination, kindness, appreciation of beauty, understanding other people, working in a team. You'll find more about them on page 77. And you can improve them, too.

FIND THE BEST TEACHING

Becoming better at something isn't *only* a matter of practising. We might practise over and over again but find we're not getting better. What has gone wrong? It's likely to be one of two things: either we need to practise differently or we need some better or different teaching. Or both!

Teaching is not simple. Sometimes, the teacher doesn't find the right way to explain something; sometimes the learner isn't ready to learn, perhaps because they need a bit more basic information first. For example, a teacher might explain a maths concept very clearly but the students whose basic maths knowledge is weaker might not grasp it, whereas others will. The teacher can't always tell who has grasped it and who is not ready to move on to the next thing. Or a student might be tired, distressed, angry, preoccupied or feeling ill and so just not take the words in.

It's really important to tell a teacher when you don't understand what they are trying to teach. And it's really important for the teacher to listen and accept and try to help. But in the real world, this isn't always easy, for many reasons: personality clashes, low mood, the behaviour of people nearby, or a whole load of things that can be going on for the student or the teacher.

ASK FOR HELP AT THE RIGHT TIME

It's important to choose the right time to approach a teacher (or any adult) for help. Here are some tips:

1. If you didn't hear something properly, ask straightaway, "Please could you repeat that?" I know this can be hard but it is important to do it if you can. It might also help other people as it's likely that you weren't the only one who didn't hear.

2. If you don't understand something first time, don't panic. Take a breath and tell yourself that you will get it. Try to work it out yourself; then, if you can't, see the next point.

3. Choose a moment when the teacher is not in a hurry. Try to decide whether your question might need a little or a lot of time. If it's a quick one, "Please could I just ask you this?" at the end of class might be fine, but otherwise try, "I'm having difficulty with this – when would be a good time to ask you about it?"

4. Remember that teachers are humans with personal lives and may have a lot to deal with apart from your problem. This does not mean you shouldn't ask them: their job is to do everything they can to help you. But do be considerate and intelligent in how and when you ask. Often a student thinks a teacher doesn't care about them if they don't reply to an email immediately, but the teacher has many students to help, as well as their own family and personal life. Teachers should not have to spend their own personal or family time on work, though they often do. So, don't be afraid to ask but do be reasonable in your expectations.

BUILD EVIDENCE OF YOUR SKILLS

When we experience proof or evidence of something, we are more inclined to trust it. As I've discussed before, praise from someone who knows us generally doesn't feel like sufficient proof. Of course, it makes us feel happy when people praise us, and praise is useful in building self-esteem. But it doesn't feel authentic enough and we are left with a sneaking suspicion that the person is just being nice because they want us to feel better. Or because they have to.

There are two forms of evidence that can work, to prove to us that we do have skills or strengths and a good chance of future success. This evidence builds our resilience by making us feel confident that even if we failed this time, we can succeed next time.

One is objective – things that come from outside our mind, physical evidence. The other is subjective – things that are generated in our own mind, after sensible thinking.

OBJECTIVE AFFIRMATION

This might include certificates, medals and prizes. Perhaps you've passed an exam in a musical instrument or you've swum a certain distance.

It also includes other things that might have no certificate or prize, but you know you did them: perhaps you performed in a play, sang in a choir, had your artwork displayed or your story read out. It isn't so important whether you think you did them really well, what matters is that you did them. They were all experiences that you had, which will have built your skills, your confidence, your knowledge about yourself.

PRACTICAL ACTIVITY

Here are some things you might have done. Record any that apply to you. Use the ideas to help you think of lots of other things, too. Then make a poster with a picture of you in the middle and illustrations (or just words) of all your achievements around you.

Sport – what sports or activities have you done? Any teams? How far can you swim? Are you better at sprinting or running a longer distance? Can you do 30 squats?

Music – played any instruments? How long for? Did you ever play in front of people? Any exams?

Singing – sung in a choir or group? Enjoy performing?

Dancing – do you enjoy creating a routine? (If you enjoy something, you're probably good at it!) Ever performed at school?

Drama – ever auditioned for anything? Performed in a school or class play?

Performance – any other performance such as speaking in public?

Art – anything displayed on a wall? What different styles can you do? Anything you feel proud of?

Schoolwork – certificates or prizes? Story read out in class? What's your best subject? What do you understand well? Do you get your homework in on time? Do you listen well? Do you put your hand up when you know the answer?

Anything else – raised money for charity, organised an event, been in charge of anything, created a surprise for someone, had an idea that other people liked, learnt all the states of the USA or capital cities around the world, dealt with an illness or injury, helped someone, dialled the emergency services, sorted out a friendship problem.

SUBJECTIVE AFFIRMATION

This requires you to think honestly about all those experiences and many more things you've done in your life, and to notice all the skills you developed during them.

For example, suppose you were involved in a school or class play. Whatever your role – on stage or behind the scenes – you learnt something during it. What? Teamwork? Leadership? Supporting others? Planning ahead? Creativity? Staying calm? Reacting under stress?

Or suppose you went on a school trip where you stayed overnight. Again, you learnt something on that trip. Maybe you developed a new friendship? Overcame a fear? Didn't feel too homesick? Overcame your homesickness? Enjoyed it more than you expected? And, again, those skills of teamwork, planning, joining in, helping others.

GROW YOUR BEST CHARACTERISTICS

Too often, when we talk about skills or strengths, we think of things that are measured by tests, certificates and competitions: things like spelling, maths, sporting skills, art, music, and any of the other subjects you learn at school and some that you might learn outside school, too, such as drama, cookery or climbing.

There's so much more to being a successful human! There are also all the values that make you the person you are. They are all worth noticing, appreciating and trying to build on – because, just like any other skills, they get better when we practise them.

These characteristics are things like:

♥ Generosity, helpfulness and kindness – being good to other people.

- ♥ Determination, perseverance, grit – not giving up.
- ♥ Teamwork, listening, sharing, leadership – how well you work with others.
- ♥ Curiosity, wanting to learn things – building your knowledge and expertise.
- ♥ Open-mindedness, tolerance – how you appreciate people who are different from you.
- ♥ Courage and willingness to have a go – being prepared to fail before you succeed.
- ♥ Creativity and inventiveness – how good you are at thinking differently and independently.
- ♥ Empathy and intuition – realising that people have different feelings and sometimes those feelings are hidden.

Which ones do you feel are your strongest traits? Recognising them will help your self-belief and these characteristics can also help you in your friendships, your work and your whole life. And, once you recognise them, you'll be motivated to find ways to keep building them.

The best way to measure your personal strengths is to use the 24 "character strengths" developed by Dr Martin Seligman, who is often called the founder of "positive psychology". He and colleagues identified these specific character strengths and developed ways of measuring and growing the characteristics so we can have better well-being and live more positive lives. On page 189 there is a link to the VIA Institute on Character website, where you'll find all 24 strengths described fully, together with a survey so that you can identify your own strongest traits. And the VIA website also has suggestions for how to build them.

PRACTICAL ACTIVITY

1. Which three or four characteristics from the list do you think are your biggest strengths? Make a poster or just a page in your notebook and write and illustrate them with the heading "My best characteristics".

2. Which one would you like to be stronger? Can you think of practical actions you could take to develop it? For example, if you think creativity isn't one of your strengths, start by collecting ideas of things you find visually appealing. Your actions could be: go to an art gallery; create a Pinterest board; borrow a book about an artist or type of art in a library. Knowing what you like is the start to creating.

Now you have lots of evidence of things you've achieved and skills and strengths you have. Take a few moments to feel proud of all you've achieved and all you can do. These skills and strengths will help you have confidence in yourself and that will make you more resilient when events happen which challenge you. You'll be able to remind yourself that although this bad thing has happened, you have all these achievements under your belt.

When you've achieved something, no one can take it away from you. Make it part of you. Own it.

USE YOUR WHOLE BRAIN

Although I said that no one can be brilliant at everything because there's not enough time in the day to practise everything to a high standard, we should still try a wide variety of activities. That way we will build all the different areas of our brain. This has several advantages:

1. We have a chance of finding new skills and pleasures that we might not have discovered otherwise.

2. Variety makes life more enjoyable.

3. Taking a break from schoolwork in order to play football or tennis (or something else) helps your brain process the schoolwork.

4. There can be a cross-over between skills. So, for example, playing sport doesn't only use physical skills but also needs teamwork, courage, sensitivity and more. One activity can improve your ability in other areas.

Every activity uses different areas of the brain. And the brain operates on a "use it or lose it" system, which means that the areas we don't use are the areas where we end up with fewer and weaker neural connections; the areas we use most end up with the most and the strongest connections.

The answer is simple: have a wide range of things you spend your time on!

PRACTICAL ACTIVITY
Write down which of these you have done in the last week:

♥ Read a book for pleasure.
♥ Drawn, painted, doodled or created any kind of art.
♥ Written something creative – a poem, letter or story.
♥ Baked or cooked.
♥ Played sport with other people.
♥ Done physical exercise.
♥ Danced.

- ♥ Played a musical instrument.
- ♥ Sung a song.
- ♥ Listened to music.
- ♥ Daydreamed.
- ♥ Typed.
- ♥ Knitted, crocheted or sewed.
- ♥ Made something.
- ♥ Solved a problem.
- ♥ Planned something.
- ♥ Concentrated very hard on one thing for an hour.
- ♥ Played a board game.
- ♥ Played a computer game.
- ♥ Walked from one place to another using a different route from usual.
- ♥ Ridden a bike or scooter.
- ♥ Performed or spoken in front of an audience.
- ♥ Learnt a new maths topic.

Be proud of all the different activities you've done: each one has helped you build skills. Your skills and achievements make you stronger and that strength gives you resilience.

Is there any type of activity that you do very little of – such as sport, art, music? Could you do something to change this?

Learning new things gives us a mental boost and builds different skills, as well as increasing confidence and self-esteem. Perfect for resilience!

REBUILD YOUR SKILLS AFTER A BAD TIME

Again, this chapter has been about building your skills so that you've got that resilience ready to help you through bad times, but there are also things you can do *after* a bad thing has happened.

My advice here is to ask yourself a small set of questions:

1. Did this bad thing happen because I lacked skills or knowledge or experience? If it did, can I improve those skills or knowledge or experience? In other words, is there anything practical I can do to make it less likely to happen again? If it was nothing to do with my skills etc. then I can relax!

2. If this bad thing is making me feel inadequate, can I focus for a while on any of my strengths so that I can see evidence that I am actually good at some things, even if one thing has just gone wrong?

3. Is this an opportunity to try something new and exciting? It might give me a boost of confidence and energy and a new set of possible strengths and skills. It might also help take my mind off the bad thing that just happened.

REFLECTION ACTIVITY

Look back to page 61 and remind yourself about Eddie, Fardin, Sadia and Mattie. Do you identify with any of them in some ways? Now that you understand more about confidence and the importance of building skills, what advice would you give each of them so that they can be more resilient to failure or difficulty? Is there one thing you would say to yourself or one thing you will do differently to help you build your own skills? My own suggestions are on page 180.

SUMMING UP

Confidence comes from the knowledge that you have skills, that you can do some things already and that you can learn more. Once you have achieved something, you know you can achieve something else. Once you have moved from not knowing or not being able to do something to being able to, you can have a growth mindset, understanding that we acquire and build skills rather than being born with them or being handed them by the good luck fairy.

Once you have the beginnings of confidence, you have the beginnings of resilience. And that confidence will be stronger when you see evidence of your abilities, rather than simply having your parents or teachers saying "good job". It's when you can say "good job" to yourself that resilience really takes off.

TOP TIPS FOR BUILDING YOUR SKILLS

1. Keep reminding yourself that the brain learns *everything* by trying and doing. We are not born able to walk: we learn to, effort by effort, stumble by stumble, step by step.

2. Don't try to be brilliant at everything: pick the things you enjoy or that appeal to you and that you think will help you.

3. Acknowledge and recognise each bit of progress and achievement along the way – you wouldn't wait until a toddler could walk perfectly before saying "well done", so don't wait until you've become perfect and brilliant at something before you praise what you've done.

4. Look at evidence of your successes. Pin certificates to your bedroom wall, make a list of tests you've passed or skills you've developed. Any time you do something you're proud

of, write it down and stick it where you can see it if you need a reminder. Notice what you *enjoy*, as this is usually a clue to things you're succeeding at.

5. Be bold and try new things every now and then: perhaps try one new activity a term or a month. Try not to be disheartened when you don't immediately feel successful but be proud when you are brave enough to keep trying. Only by trying will you give yourself the chance to succeed and improve.

DIARY TIME

Here are some things you could record in your diary, as well as the practical activities:

1. Two or three things you remember from this chapter.

2. Did you identify or empathise with any of the imaginary characters at the start of this chapter?

3. Your goals for tomorrow, this week and this term.

4. What one thing would you most love to be better at? What steps could you take to make that happen? Can you turn this into a resolution that is realistic and practical?

5. Look back at the material about characteristics on page 77. You wrote down what you felt were your best strengths. Now write an example of how you used or demonstrated each one.

CHAPTER FOUR:
BUILD YOUR POSITIVE COPING STRATEGIES

HOW DOES THIS HELP RESILIENCE?

Difficult times and negative emotions can drag us down and weaken us if we're not careful. Coping strategies are among our most important tools and if we use the right ones we feel stronger and are better able to deal with whatever problem comes along next. That's resilience.

The good news is that we instinctively do things to reduce our pain, so you are probably already using some coping strategies without thinking about them. The bad news is that some of the things we instinctively do are not healthy or useful so, although they might feel good at the time, they are not beneficial strategies. Your resilience will be stronger if you use positive strategies but not if you use negative ones. This chapter is about telling the difference and building the positive ones.

TEENAGE EXAMPLES

Let's look at these characters and see what they are doing to deal with pain or difficulty. You might notice that some of them are not using good coping strategies.

♥♥♥

Naomi is a talented gymnast and has won a few medals at competitions over the years. But about three months ago she wasn't feeling well and had two bad competitions in a row, scoring poorly. Her coach told her not to worry and that she'd get her form back but Naomi was really upset by these "failures" and now believes that she's lost her edge. She feels that her body is changing and she just can't do it any more. She was entered for another competition, and she became more and more nervous as the day approached. Luckily, on the morning of the competition, she woke with a bit of a sore throat so she told her mum she didn't feel well enough to go. A similar thing happened the next time, too, when Naomi woke up with a headache. She got ready for the competition but was looking so white-faced that her mum said she shouldn't go. Thing is, Naomi recovered from both the sore throat and the headache really quickly, so then she felt bad – but still relieved that she hadn't had to do the competition. There's another one coming up: maybe she'll be able to get out of it again.

♥♥♥

Ollie is a healthy, active fifteen year old who does well at school, both in the classroom and in most sports. He's the best swimmer in his year and one of the fastest long-distance runners. His problem is that he's worried about his parents. They both have very stressful jobs with long hours: his mother is a senior doctor in a hospital and his father is a head teacher. You'd think with jobs like that they'd both know that drinking is not a good way to deal with stress. And they do know it, but this knowledge doesn't stop them coming home from work and saying things like "God, I need a drink" and then having quite a bit more than one. Ollie isn't going to drink like that: he wants to be the healthiest he can be and he loves the feeling of his body getting stronger and fitter. When Ollie is feeling stressed or worried about something, he goes for a run: all his tensions and worries just disappear and he comes back feeling better. It helps him sleep, too.

♥♥♥

Ollie's pretty annoyed with his friend Pavel right now. Pavel used to like the same things as Ollie: he'd always come and play any sport or join after-school activities, especially outdoor ones. But now Pavel has joined the smokers – the same kids Ollie and Pavel had looked down on in earlier years, the ones who just messed about and never tried to succeed. Pavel's parents split up recently and Pavel changed a lot after that. Ollie tried to distract him and take his mind off the problems at home – they even had plans to create a comic together as Pavel was brilliant at drawing – but Pavel just wanted to stay in his room and play games with his headphones on so he could block everything out. Then, the smoking started. Ollie said: "What are you doing that for, mate? And hanging out with those idiots!" And Pavel snapped back: "You don't know anything about them. Go back to your perfect life!"

Naomi, Ollie, his parents and his friend Pavel are all doing things in response to stresses and problems in their lives, but only Ollie is making a healthy choice: going for a run when he wants to deal with stress. The others are making negative, unhealthy choices. Naomi is avoiding challenges because she's too nervous; so, although she's avoided distress, she's also missing opportunities to enjoy success and feel proud of herself, which would make her stronger for the next time. Ollie's parents are using alcohol and Pavel is smoking. They like the temporary feeling it gives them but are ignoring the many health problems that will follow. It's very easy to start using such negative coping strategies without even realising, but we need to notice when we're doing that and find positive ones instead. It isn't always easy, especially if the habit is a strong one, but it's always possible. Sometimes with help.

WHAT ARE COPING STRATEGIES?

Everyone has coping strategies – babies, children, teenagers and adults of all ages. They are a survival instinct to try to reduce distress. So, a small baby cries when hungry, thirsty, cold, hot or uncomfortable, because this brings a solution: an adult to sort the problem. That's the baby's best – or only – coping strategy because the baby can't do anything for itself and the result is that the problem is sorted.

If older humans cry because they're hungry or have any other simple need, this is *not* the best coping strategy because we can sort the problem ourselves: eat something if we're hungry, for example. Crying in that situation could also have negative consequences: people will be annoyed and criticise us for not being able to do such a simple thing ourselves. If we can't do it ourselves because we're injured or some other good reason, crying still isn't *usually* the best strategy; the best strategy is to ask for help. (Crying *can* be a good coping strategy sometimes, though! See the section on positive coping strategies.)

As we grow from being a baby into childhood, adolescence and adulthood, we learn many other ways to deal with problems – everything from a bad day at school to a major setback or a really awful situation. If we choose positive strategies, we will directly improve our resilience, building a shield around us which will allow us to face the world strongly, without hiding from it. First, then, we need to know what the negative strategies are, so we can avoid them.

NEGATIVE COPING STRATEGIES

All coping strategies give some relief from a problem but some have longer-term negative consequences. People use such negative strategies because they enjoy the short-term relief from distress; they might not think about the long-term results. Most people know they're not really good ways to deal with bad times but distress stops them thinking straight or being able to control their actions. They might not realise that what they're doing is likely to weaken their resilience. Soon the action becomes a habit: the easy thing to do but not the best thing.

Part of being resilient involves learning and using lots of positive strategies, so we need to know what the negative ones are before we can avoid them. Then we can make the right choices and build resilience.

Here are some examples of negative coping strategies. You'll see that some are more problematic than others.

- ♥ **Biting fingernails or the skin around them** – People who do this tend to do it more when they are stressed; it is a habit which gives very short-term relief but it might be painful or look unpleasant. It's not as much of a problem as some of the other actions people take but most people who bite their nails wish they didn't.

- ♥ **Self-harming** – People sometimes cause physical pain or damage to themselves as a way to deal with emotional pain, but afterwards this is very distressing and can be dangerous. Usually people don't really think this is going to make their problems go away, but the short-term is what they focus on.

- ♥ **Smoking tobacco** – Nicotine and some other chemicals in cigarettes can make people feel relaxed for a short while, but there are serious risks to many aspects of health in the short and long term.

- ♥ **Alcohol** – As with smoking tobacco. And there are immediate severe dangers when you are drunk.

- ♥ **Drugs** – Both illegal drugs and some prescription medicines – as with alcohol and tobacco. (Note that occasionally a doctor might prescribe pills for anxiety and various mental health problems. Always follow your doctor's advice and take the medication as prescribed, but your doctor should review this regularly, as some pills should only be taken for a short while, and others must be reduced gradually.) No one thinks that smoking, drinking or taking drugs will actually cure their problems but they often do these things to get away from bad feelings. This will make them less resilient.

- **Problematic eating habits and eating disorders** – There are many sorts of specific eating disorders, with anorexia nervosa and bulimia being the best known. There's also a broader category of "disordered eating", which describes people with an unhealthy mental attitude towards food and exercise, who feel a lot of guilt around food and will often restrict what they eat. Sometimes people start these behaviours believing that it will cure their problems – for example, they might think that if they were thinner they would be happier – but by the time they discover that they aren't happier, the habits can be too deep to change easily.

- **Avoiding the thing you're worried or distressed about** – If something causes us pain or distress it's natural that we try to avoid it. And sometimes that's the right thing to do: it's sensible to avoid feeling very sad by not reading sad stories, for example, or to choose not to go on a roller-coaster if we find them terrifying. But if the thing that causes us distress is something that would benefit us – such as speaking in public, meeting new people, going to school, or entering a competition where we might do well and feel proud – then it's not useful to avoid it. Also, if we have a phobia, treatment involves helping us feel less afraid of the trigger by gently increasing exposure to it, rather than complete avoidance. So, avoidance is generally not a good way to deal with difficult things – it's a negative coping strategy.

If you are using any of these negative coping strategies, you might need help to stop. Do talk to a trusted adult or ask to see your doctor, who will be able to point you in the right direction. As I say, these things can become habits. Habits are often hard to break but not impossible.

Soon we are going to look at all the wonderful positive strategies you could use but first let's understand what stress is and the problems it can sometimes cause.

UNDERSTAND STRESS

Although stress on its own is not a problem, repeated stresses, without good strategies to deal with this, can chip away at your ability to bounce back from problems. So, when we talk about managing stress, we really mean minimising or avoiding any negative effects of repeated stress. Stress management is therefore a really important part of resilience. The good news is that there are lots of simple, practical things you can do to keep problems away.

What is stress? We talk about "stress" a lot, and almost always in a negative way, but it's important to understand that it is actually a positive biological process, evolved in all animals to help us survive and succeed. The "stress response" happens instantly when the brain detects any kind of threat: before we even know what the threat is, the brain triggers the "fight, flight or freeze" response, so that our body is able to super-perform in order to beat the threat. When Homo sapiens first existed – more than 200,000 years ago – this response evolved for the threats we faced then: lions, snakes, enemies. We have some different specific threats nowadays but we still react with fear to any animal that might harm us, any stranger (because they might be dangerous) and any situation where we are under pressure to perform, whether mentally or physically.

The stress response involves the hormones adrenalin and cortisol flooding our body with several instant effects: our heart rate and breathing speed up (sending extra oxygen and energy to the large muscles we might need to use); our muscles tense up, ready to spring into action; and our brain focuses very intently on the thing that threatens us, ignoring other things. We feel anxious and alert.

This means we can super-perform. When I was chased by a goose at the age of thirteen, I leapt over a massive gate: I could never have done that if I hadn't been anxious about the threat.

So, stress is not bad: it's welcome and beneficial. It is there to help you win races and matches and competitions, ace your exams, do your best stage performance, make a brilliant speech. And to keep you safe from harm, just as it would have done 200,000 years ago.

But stress does bring problems and can wear away our resilience. If we have a lot of stress, it can dominate our life, leaving no time or energy or brain bandwidth for facing the future with a resilient mindset. Too much stress can make us underperform instead of super-perform. We need to understand the possible problems so we can look out for them and build strategies against them. We can learn to deal with plenty of stress in our lives *and* build our resilience to future stress.

The problems that stress can bring are:

- ♥ We might feel *too* anxious. Our stress response can make us feel so uncomfortable that we panic and can only think about how bad we feel, not what we need to do.

- ♥ We might feel anxious at times when we need to relax: for example, when trying to sleep.

- ♥ We might feel anxious too often. Cortisol takes longer to disappear than adrenalin, so if we have lots of stresses it can build up. Cortisol build-up causes lots of problems: loss of sleep, poor concentration, low mood, poor immune system.

Those problems can be short term – when something specific and temporary is happening – or long term. When they are long term this can be more of a problem, because you might get so used to being stressed that you don't even recognise that you are.

It's important to recognise a very wide range of emotions or circumstances which can be part of stress, including: anxiety, distress, fear, overwork, change, powerlessness, shame, guilt and feeling that people are looking at you.

A WORD ABOUT PANIC ATTACKS

A panic attack is an extremely unpleasant experience. When someone has a panic attack they often think they must be about to die. This is the panic talking as they are not actually going to die.

Symptoms include the following (but each individual might not have all of these):

- ❤ Racing heart.
- ❤ Very fast breathing.
- ❤ Sweating.
- ❤ Desperate need to run away or leave the room.
- ❤ Feeling of shock and terror.

Panic attacks are an extreme response to anxiety. They usually pass quickly, especially if the person can use simple calming techniques such as belly breathing (see page 95). But once someone has had one they might be afraid that it will happen again. So if you've had one it makes sense to learn some strategies in advance. It's also important to tell close friends how to help you if it happens: to get you to focus on slowing your breathing and to keep reassuring you that no, you are not going to die.

If you keep having panic attacks, do see a doctor. It's possible you would benefit from medical help and a doctor can point you in the right direction.

WHAT ARE THE SIGNS THAT YOU ARE SUFFERING FROM STRESS?

Part of building coping strategies to be resilient against bad things happening in your life is to be aware of the signs that stress is undermining your well-being. Everyone has different signs. You might have one or several of these:

- ♥ Frequent headaches.
- ♥ Frequent stomach aches.
- ♥ Pains in the muscles of your shoulders, neck and jaw.
- ♥ Feeling dizzy.
- ♥ Feeling nauseous.
- ♥ Problems sleeping.
- ♥ Feeling nervous without knowing why.
- ♥ Often crying for small reasons.
- ♥ Changes in appetite – increased or reduced appetite.
- ♥ Mood swings and snappiness.
- ♥ Chest pains.

Of course, any of these *can* be caused by something other than stress and you should get anything you're worried about checked out by a doctor. But these are also all very commonly simply caused by stress.

PRACTICAL ACTIVITY

What do you think are your own signs of stress? Draw a simple picture to represent yourself and label it with any signs or symptoms that you sometimes get when you are anxious, stressed, nervous or dealing with worry.

Knowing that these are most likely to be normal stress symptoms can help you stop worrying about them. If you aren't sure whether something is a sign of stress, ask a trusted adult. If necessary you can get reassurance from your doctor. Then you'll be ready to use some of the positive strategies you'll learn now. This will help you cope next time stress affects you: you will be becoming resilient by learning good coping actions and creating healthy habits of self-care.

POSITIVE COPING STRATEGIES

Now we can look at positive coping strategies. You don't have to use them all but do read them all so that you know what might help. Then choose which you'd like to try, but remember that there's nothing which will remove all your stress immediately and permanently: even the most effective strategies have to be repeated as often as needed.

BELLY BREATHING

This is a brilliant quick strategy which everyone should learn! It's an ideal emergency technique. Even people who are normally relaxed can have an episode of stress, which can arrive without warning, so do have this trick up your sleeve.

Here's how it works. The body's normal reaction to stress makes our breathing faster and shallower, using the upper chest rather than the whole of our lungs. This is fine when we really need to spring into action immediately but it happens far more often than that and in situations where it is not necessary. We need to spot this type of breathing and change it.

You can check whether your breathing is relaxed or stressed right now. Place one hand on your upper chest, just below your throat, and the other on your abdomen, your "belly", just under your rib cage. Keep breathing normally for a while and notice which hand is moving more. If it's your upper hand, your breathing is somewhat stressed; if it's the hand on your belly that moves more, your breathing is nice and relaxed.

So, belly breathing basically involves shifting your breathing down so that your belly moves more than your upper chest.

You'll find lots of videos online showing you how to do it, and there's a free audio on my website, but here's a simple description:

1. Sit or lie comfortably. You may have your eyes open or closed, as you wish. Many people find it easier at first with eyes closed.

2. Breathe in through your nose to the count of three, then hold for the count of four and breathe out through your mouth for the count of seven. (Use the word "chimpanzee" so that you do this at the right speed: "One chimpanzee, two chimpanzees" etc.)

3. Do this for a few breaths until you've got the rhythm; then continue but focus your mind on your belly moving out as you breathe.

4. Each breath you take, think about softening and relaxing the muscles of your shoulders and stomach area; each breath a little softer, more relaxed, heavier.

5. Continue doing this as long as you want.

In an emergency, when you might not have time to do all that, simply tell yourself, "Breathe so that my belly moves and let my shoulder, neck and abdominal muscles become loose and relaxed." It's a simple shift of your breathing from upper chest to belly: belly breathing.

Do it when you're in bed wanting to sleep, too. It's a really useful way to take your mind off worries and help your mind become calm.

PRACTICAL ACTIVITY

Before you go to bed this evening, practise belly breathing. Find a demonstration on the internet or the free relaxation audio on my website. Make sure you won't be disturbed for up to fifteen minutes and find a place to sit or lie safely and listen to the instructions.

PRACTICAL SELF-CARE – THE TABLE OF WELL-BEING

One of the first things I talked about in this book was the importance of caring about yourself, being your own supporter. You might not think that looking after yourself requires *skills* but think about it: some people seem to look after themselves better than others, so there must be something we can learn, build and improve.

The image that I use is the "four-legged table of well-being". The four legs represent: food and water, exercise, sleep, relaxation. The thing about a four-legged table is that if three legs are strong and one is weak and breaks, the whole table collapses. We need to look after *all four legs*.

Think about how you can do that every day. You might not

be able to work on all of them equally every day but keep an eye on which of the four legs might be suffering a bit and take steps to strengthen it.

Here are some tips. You'll find resources for all of them on page 187, including my own books and website.

Food and water

- ♥ Don't go hungry – if you're hungry, your brain won't be able to make good decisions or focus.
- ♥ Eat a varied diet – the best way to know that you're getting all the fabulous nutrients that make us healthy is to eat lots of different things.
- ♥ Enjoy lots of fruit and vegetables.
- ♥ Eat plenty of beans, grains (e.g. oats), seeds and nuts (if not allergic).
- ♥ Only have sugary items and highly processed food as occasional treats.
- ♥ Don't count calories, count variety.
- ♥ Drink enough – aim to drink sufficient water that you don't become thirsty. Avoid: fizzy or sugary drinks; energy drinks; alcohol (obviously); and too much caffeine.

Exercise

- ♥ Be active – walk when you can, rather than going by car; get off the bus a stop early; take the stairs, not the lift; get up and get moving every hour if you've been sitting down.
- ♥ Go with what you enjoy – if you don't like team sport, do something on your own; discover whether you like short, fast exercise or longer, slower exercise.

- Exercise with someone else to motivate you.
- Do an activity that raises your heart rate and makes you a bit out of breath for at least 30 minutes three or four times a week.
- Don't exercise to lose weight – exercise to be healthy and strong.

Sleep

- Everyone's sleep needs are different but most people aged 11–25 feel and perform best when they have between 7.5 and 9 hours of sleep a night; *almost everyone* is negatively affected if they regularly have fewer than six hours a night.
- Aim to go to bed and wake up at roughly the same time each night and morning.
- During the one or two hours before you turn your light off, make sure you're doing gentle, calming activities that help your body wind down and your brain understand that it's nearly bedtime.
- During that time, avoid activities that raise alertness and heart rate: caffeine, stress, exercise, daylight, bright lights, screens and messages.
- Learn some techniques for those nights when sleep doesn't come easily. See the resources for references to detailed advice.

Relaxation

- Understand that stress is something that helps us perform but we also need to keep it under control. (There's more on this on page 91.)
- Believe that "relaxation is not a luxury" – it's not something you give yourself as a "reward" when you deserve it but

something that improves well-being and health.

- ♥ Learn a breathing exercise such as belly breathing. You'll find one in the resources and I talk about it on page 95.

- ♥ Build small relaxation breaks into every day, especially during times when you are extra busy and stressed. You'll find more about this below, including how to choose suitable activities according to your mental needs.

- ♥ Have a hobby. This will be something you can turn to when you need to disengage your brain from what you're working on and free it for a different type of activity.

Remember, looking after yourself builds your physical and mental health, which makes resilience easier.

PRACTICAL ACTIVITY

Draw a picture of a table with four legs. Give each leg one of these labels: food and water, exercise, sleep, relaxation. Beneath or alongside each leg, write or draw one or more things that you have done in the last 24 hours that you think was a positive action for that leg. Is there one leg that you feel is not as strong as it could be for you? Can you think of or investigate one or two actions you could take to improve it?

BUILDING RELAXATION INTO YOUR DAY

Above, you learnt that relaxation is not a luxury but essential for well-being. It is one of the most important and most enjoyable positive coping strategies. When people are feeling overwhelmed by stress or a difficult time, they often think that the simple act of taking a break couldn't possibly help. But each tiny act is like a building block: one step at a time, you can reduce your stress and become better able to face your challenges.

When should you relax? There are two equally good times: a) when you are actually feeling stressed and b) any time! Sometimes we can't take a break when we feel stressed, because we have to deal with a specific situation, but we should then promise ourselves that later that day we will do something relaxing. Even having that to look forward to can make a difference.

How long should you relax for? However long you feel you need and can manage. Many relaxation activities can be very short indeed. Some of the suggestions that follow only need a few minutes.

Quick ideas

★ *Stroke a pet.*
★ *Doodle.*
★ *Do a quick puzzle or a few minutes of a jigsaw.*
★ *Have a drink of chilled water with a mint leaf or lemon slice.*
★ *Have a snack if you're hungry.*
★ *Lie on the grass or sand.*
★ *Go outside for a fast ten-minute walk.*
★ *Massage your hands or temples.*
★ *Smell something gorgeous.*
★ *Video message a friend.*
★ *Write a kind note to a grandparent, other relative or friend.*
★ *Learn a new word.*
★ *Daydream — what would you do with a lottery win or three wishes?*
★ *Light a scented candle.*
★ *Quick mindfulness — see page 113; and whichever of the activities you choose from this list, do it "mindfully", properly focusing on the activity.*

Longer ideas

★ Read a book.

★ Have a soak in the bath.

★ Do any sport.

★ Watch any sport.

★ Walk – on your own or with others; it could be a fast power-walk or a gentle stroll .

★ Swim or run.

★ Go to the cinema.

★ Go for a coffee or ice-cream – with a friend or alone.

★ Bake or cook – or plan something to bake or cook.

★ Make a snowman or sandcastle or daisy chain.

★ Draw a picture.

★ Write a poem.

★ Write a letter to a relative.

★ Tidy your bedroom.

★ Plan a get-together or party.

★ Engage in any hobby – maybe a new one.

MAKE THE RIGHT CHOICE FOR THE RIGHT SITUATION

Although any of those ideas (and many others you might think of) can work well as a relaxation activity, it's important to choose the right one at the right time. There are two types of feeling stressed and some relaxation activities will work well for one but not the other.

Think about which of these applies more to you at the moment:

1. You feel generally anxious, tense and nervous and want to feel calmer, more relaxed.

2. You have a big worry preoccupying your thoughts and you want to take your mind off it.

If you identify with the first category, you'll find things like walking, swimming, lying on the grass or sand, or listening to music all really helpful. But if you have something big on your mind, you'll probably find those things won't help. The reason is that those things take very little concentration – "brain bandwidth" – leaving plenty left to carry on worrying. So, to take your mind off a worry, you'll need something that takes a lot of attention: playing sport with other people, watching a film, reading an engaging book, doing a puzzle or playing a computer game, for example.

When you look back at the relaxation activities I suggested, you'll notice that some use very little concentration, such as walking, and others use a lot, such as reading a book. Think about which one will be best for you at this time.

IS PLAYING A COMPUTER GAME A POSITIVE STRATEGY?

It might or might not be! There are three things to consider:

1. Does it *really* make you feel relaxed? If so, it's fine. But if it actually makes you tense or stressed, it could be a negative coping strategy.

2. Can you easily restrict yourself to just 30 minutes and not be tempted keep playing? If so, fine. If not, that suggests you're not in control, perhaps even somewhat addicted. Then it becomes a negative strategy.

3. Are you also spending an appropriate amount of time doing these things: night-time sleep, face-to-face time with people, healthy eating, physical activity and other non-screen hobbies or relaxation activities? If so, fine. If not, your computer gaming is perhaps taking more time than it should.

PRACTICAL ACTIVITY

Make a poster with all the relaxation activities you can think of that you like to do and have the opportunity to do. Include things that are quick and others that take longer. Make sure they are varied – exciting and relaxing, outdoor and indoor, with or without friends, challenging and easy. And make sure that some use a little concentration (for when you just need to feel calmer) and others use a lot (for when you need to take your mind off something). Decorate your poster however you like and pin it to your wall.

BE ACTIVE

There is so much science to prove that physical activity is a wonderful positive coping strategy. It's good for stress, confidence, skills, self-esteem and mood. It also helps sleep and learning. Unfortunately, some people don't like it – or haven't found a form of activity they like. Also, of course, if you think you're not good at sport or anything involving moving your body, or if you hate people seeing your body, exercise could have a negative effect: making you feel bad about yourself. If you identify with this, there are lots of ideas on the pages that follow. There's something for everyone.

Because we know the vast benefits, physically and mentally, and because these have great potential for boosting resilience (by improving mental health, confidence and skills) it's really important that everyone can find at least one physical activity that *will* make them feel good about themselves.

If you are someone who likes being active, you won't have difficulty thinking of more things to try and to spend your active time on. If you aren't, you will need some simple, attractive advice.

As you will imagine, I have some!

First, sit less

There's lots of evidence that sitting down for too long is bad for our health. Of course, some people have a physical reason which means they have to sit down – but that's a special situation. I'm talking about people who *can* stand up and move around but who spend a lot of time sitting.

You don't have to play sport every day: you just have to remind yourself to get up and move around every now and then. You could set an hourly timer to remind you.

Second, choose to use your feet

Small amounts of extra activity will add up without you noticing the effort. You won't have to change your clothes because you're not going to get hot and sweaty. For example, instead of going your whole journey on a bus, get off two stops earlier – or three, or four, or walk the whole way. When there's a lift, take the stairs. When there's a short walk, take a longer route. (Of course, follow appropriate safety guidelines.)

You have probably heard that 10,000 steps is the target we should be aiming for every day. There's actually no evidence that this is the magic ideal number of steps: it's just a nice round number and is believed to be a reasonable goal. But if you only do 8000 that's better than 4000. You can buy a cheap step counter or you might have one on your phone and it can be fun to try to achieve that target. You'll probably find on a normal school day you do that easily, especially if you're active at break time, walk at least part of the way to school or have a PE lesson, for example.

Don't become obsessive, though. This is about a healthy, reasonable lifestyle, not an obsession with exercise.

Third, know yourself

Work out what you don't like about physical activity. It could be any (or many) of the following:

- ♥ You don't like being hot and sweaty.
- ♥ There is a physical reason why some movements are painful or difficult.
- ♥ You don't want people to see parts of your body that are usually covered.
- ♥ You hate changing rooms and communal showering.
- ♥ You don't like team games.
- ♥ You don't like competition.
- ♥ You think everyone is better than you.
- ♥ You find it boring.

I understand all those reasons and I identify with most of them myself. But whoever you are, there *is* something you could enjoy. As a young person, you don't always have the full range of choice; some activities also depend where you live; and some cost money (though many don't). But I do believe there is something you could do which, even if you don't love it at the time, you won't *hate* and you'll be pleased you made the effort for. (That's like me with running: I don't love actually doing it but I love *having done* it and the feeling carries me through the whole day.)

Here are some suggestions:

- ♥ If you prefer exercising on your own, try swimming, walking or running. (I know there are likely to be other people in a swimming pool but try to ignore them; choose a time when there are few people and mostly adults, because you are less likely to feel they are judging you.) If you choose to exercise alone, don't put yourself in danger. Tell an adult where you're going. Be wise.

- ♥ If you'd like to exercise in your room, with no one seeing, try dancing to your favourite music, or using online aerobics, yoga or fitness videos.
- ♥ If you don't want to get hot and sweaty, try yoga or Pilates. (Again, classes can be online.)
- ♥ If you have a disability or pain, a physiotherapist can show you activities you can do.
- ♥ If you want to enjoy outdoor activity with other people but without playing a game or showing up things you feel weak in, try geocaching or a treasure hunt or go on an expedition with your family or friends. You could go to a local tourist attraction, such as a castle – great for steps!
- ♥ Give something a try once or twice, to test it out. Look on your local library's website or noticeboard and join with a good friend, ideally someone else who feels nervous or reluctant.

Don't make things too hard for yourself or it will be difficult to stick at it. When I started running, having not really wanted or planned to, I did the Couch to 5k programme, which is notoriously organised in very easy steps. Even I could do it and I'm still running years later.

Doing regular physical activity not only helps deal with stress: it gives you skills, too. Win-win!

FIND THE THING YOU CAN CONTROL

Very often we spend too much time focusing on the wrong things: the things we can't do anything about. We fret about the past: "Why did I say that? Why couldn't I have done that instead? If only I'd ..." And we worry about the future: "What if I get ill? What if I fail all my exams? What if someone I love dies?"

Sometimes, it's useful to think about such things – a bit. It can be useful to go over something bad that happened and work out why and to think whether there was anything we could have done to prevent it. It can even be helpful occasionally to think through how we'd feel and act if something awful happened in the future: it's a bit like having a bad dream – it can be a useful way of processing a normal fear. But when we spend so much time worrying about these things that we can't enjoy the present or do sensible, practical things which might help our future, then we've wasted our time.

So, when it feels as though something bad is happening which you can't control, find the part you can control and focus on that. Supposing your grandma is ill: you can't prevent that, but you can make her feel happy by drawing her a picture, or writing a poem or a joke, or baking a cake, or recording a video for her. Supposing you've missed some schoolwork through illness and you think you're going to fail your exams: you can't do anything about the fact that you were ill, but you can ask a teacher to help you find ways to catch up as well as possible.

"WHAT WENT WELL?"

This is a well-used technique which was first described and researched by psychologist Martin Seligman. It's sometimes known as the "Three Blessings" exercise.

You just take a few minutes at the end of each day to acknowledge three things that went well for you that day. Write them down and spend a little time thinking about them and how you felt when they happened. It doesn't matter if it's things you did or things that happened to you.

The things could be as small as "It was sunny this morning", "I walked to school instead of getting a lift", "I finished my work in time", "I enjoyed my lunch", "I made Dad a cup of tea" or "I remembered to wish James a happy birthday". Or they could be bigger things, such as "I answered two questions in class", "I got a good mark in a test", "I scored a goal", "I finished reading a book", "Mrs Bright said I'd worked hard", "My brother didn't tease me", "I had fun with Sophie". Or, on a really good day, it could be much bigger and more noticeable things, such as winning a prize, coming top in a test, being picked for a team.

If you are feeling down or anxious it can often be difficult to think of good things. I urge you to give yourself a chance and really try. It could be that you are reluctant to allow yourself to feel happy. If that's how you feel and if you've had this feeling for a couple of weeks now, I encourage you to talk to an adult about it in case you are suffering a condition such as depression, which makes it very hard to see the positive things in your life.

Doing the "What went well" activity regularly does help. It allows you to see the good things in your life while not ignoring the bad. And each positive thought or moment helps strengthen your mood and your ability to withstand tough times.

GIVE YOURSELF A WORRY SLOT

Is there something your mind keeps coming back to, a recurring negative thought or anxiety? If it's something genuinely relevant to your life at the moment – such as exams, or a real worry about someone in your family or any specific thing that's hard for you right now – it's fine and healthy to spend *some* time thinking about it. But not if it takes over your life. So, give yourself a short slot in the day when you are allowed to worry about and even be upset about it, so long as you don't do this during the lead-up to sleep or during the night.

When it's outside your worry slot, firmly push the thought away.

BREAK THE WORRY CHAIN

Worries or negative thoughts or experiences have a habit of triggering other worries, especially in people who are more anxious than others. Perhaps you have a particular recurring fear – let's say about getting ill – but you haven't been thinking about it for a while so it's not a problem. Then a worry about failing an exam comes along. This triggers your worry about getting ill and any other worries you sometimes have. Worries are linked – which is why I call this a worry chain – and when you're in an anxious state all the worries at the back of your mind come flooding to the front.

The key is first to recognise that this is what is happening: "Here come my old worries because something has set them off again." Then you can tell yourself to use one of your positive strategies to help deal with it. Mindfulness – which you can read about on page 112 – can be very good for this. Or it could be that you make extra effort to concentrate on your work or a physical activity, or you go out and have a good time with friends. You're recognising that you're vulnerable now and you're taking steps to be resilient.

CHANGE YOUR MIND

Do you sometimes find that a negative thought keeps going over and over in your mind? It might be to do with a mistake you made; a bad thing that happened; a "what if that happened?" type of worry; or a negative belief about yourself, such as "I'm stupid/unpopular/unlucky/overweight/unworthy". It dominates your thinking for a while – minutes or hours or days. Perhaps it keeps you awake at night.

This negative thought is simply a pathway or network of pathways in your brain which you have created yourself, even though you didn't mean to. Every time we have a thought it makes a pathway in the brain, which means it's easier to have that thought again. Each time you repeat the thought you make the pathway stronger and easier to follow again.

That's how you create a "thought habit". Just like biting your fingernails or fiddling with your hair or clicking a pen, it becomes something you do, but in your mind instead of elsewhere in your body.

If this sounds familiar, it's time to create a different pathway in your brain, a new and positive thought habit!

All you have to do is choose a different thought to fight the negative one. "I'm useless" could become "X might think I'm useless but I'm not" or "I am good at plenty of things and those are the things that matter". "I'm overweight" can become "My body gives me my life and I'm going to look after it and make it healthy" or "I love how I felt when I walked fast for half an hour".

I'm not suggesting this is easy: it will certainly take some time and practice. We seem to find it easier to believe negative thoughts than positive ones so it might take many repetitions of your positive ideas before you genuinely start to believe them.

Do also revisit Chapter Three and remind yourself about how we need evidence to prove to ourselves that we can do things. You'll also find a link on page 189 to an item on my website called the "Pathways Exercise".

MINDFULNESS OR MEDITATION

There are different forms of meditation but they all involve methods of controlling one's mind and body in order to reach a state of deep relaxation. It is difficult and requires practice, although there are simpler exercises anyone can try.

Mindfulness is one type of meditation. It helps you to be "in the moment", focusing on the little details of what you are doing, sensing and feeling *now*. If other thoughts come into your mind you may acknowledge them but then let them pass out of your mind and not dominate you or spoil your relaxation.

Mindfulness has become popular and there are many simple ways you can bring some of its ideas into daily life. For example, supposing you have an apple or an ice cream or a glass of iced water or anything delicious. You could take a mouthful and properly stop to notice – be mindful of – everything about it: the sensation in each part of your mouth, the texture, taste and smell, how it feels as it goes down your throat. You'd think of all your senses and everything you can notice.

Mindfulness can help you slow down when your mind and body are racing and things feel overwhelming. It doesn't work for everyone, though. So, if you try it and it doesn't work for you or you find it annoying, this does not mean there's something wrong with you! It doesn't work for me either. Maybe I don't have patience and maybe I should try harder, but I know that different things work better for me and those are the things I'd rather do.

PRACTICAL ACTIVITY

Choose a familiar activity that you normally do without thinking. Examples might be: eating, getting dressed, showering, doing your hair or putting on make-up, making a cup of tea, walking up the stairs, travelling to school. Instead of doing it without thinking, do it mindfully – in other words, focus as much of your attention as possible on this familiar activity, noticing and thinking about every tiny aspect of it, how your body is moving and feeling, what you can smell, see, hear, feel, taste.

For example, suppose you are eating a piece of toast: notice its colour and smell; see the patterns of seeds or which bits are more golden than others; how does it feel in your hand and on your lips? As you bite into it, close your eyes and pause to notice everything about taste, smell, texture. Count how many times you chew each mouthful. What does your jaw feel like as it moves? Where did this bread come from? Who might have made it?

You just slowed down your thinking and directed your mind in a gentle, calming way, away from the stressful, hectic demands of your life. You gave your stress response a break. By allowing that tiny space to breathe and relax, you used a healthy, positive coping strategy which you can use many times to calm yourself down and give your mind a chance to grow strong and controlled.

TALK TO SOMEONE

You've heard the phrase, "A worry shared is a worry halved". It really is true. But you have to pick the right person and the right time. Think about your support network – see Chapter Two – and work out who you'd most like to tell about a particular anxiety you have. Maybe it's someone who has been through something similar or just someone who is good at listening.

Sometimes, they might not be able to help immediately. Perhaps they were worried about something themselves and couldn't listen. Perhaps they just didn't manage to say the right thing or didn't know what to say.

Then you might turn to someone else. Or you might notice that actually you feel better anyway, just for having talked it through with someone.

BE THE FRIEND IN YOUR HEAD

Talking to yourself as though you were your own best friend (as you should be!) is a great coping strategy. Some people have conversations in their own head and this is perfectly OK. Sometimes you might even find yourself doing it out loud. Lots of sports people do this to encourage themselves. "Come on – you can do this!" is an obvious example.

SEEK PROFESSIONAL HELP

Sometimes you need to talk to a professional, rather than someone close to you. Professionals such as doctors, therapists and counsellors are trained in various ways to help people suffering from a range of problems such as depression, anxiety, eating disorders and obsessive behaviour. All the advice in this book will help protect you against any such problems and anything else that makes your mind a difficult place to be, but there are times when my advice won't be enough and you might need help from someone trained to help you towards individual solutions. Some therapists can change how your thoughts affect you and help you think and react in different ways.

These are the times when you should seek professional help:

♥ If you have been feeling low for a couple of weeks, especially if there isn't an obvious cause; perhaps there's a feeling of dullness or sadness that you just can't shake off.

♥ If your anxieties or obsessive thoughts are spoiling your ability to live a full life – for example, your fears are stopping you joining in things with your friends or family, or are disrupting your school work or social life.

♥ If you have had more than one panic attack – see page 93.

♥ If you don't know who to turn to with your problems.

♥ If you think you have signs of any type of eating disorder – see the Resources section on page 187 for websites which will help you know.

♥ If you ever think about suicide or that it would be better if you didn't exist. If you have these thoughts, don't delay: tell an adult and arrange to see a medical professional as soon as possible.

The best place to start is usually your family doctor but you can also use the contact options on the websites of major charities, such as Childline or the Samaritans. You can also ask any trusted adult for advice about where to turn.

GET RELIABLE INFORMATION

It's a good coping strategy to turn to information to help with a problem. But how can you know what information to trust? Even experts sometimes disagree with each other. Science isn't always about things that have been proven to be true: science is about discovering, questioning, analysing, working things out and sharing the best information we have at this moment.

The coronavirus pandemic produced plenty of examples of experts disagreeing and intelligent people coming to different conclusions about which information to believe and which advice to follow. This sometimes made people panic instead of working out what they could control and how best to face the future strongly. When people didn't know what was reliable or chose the wrong information to believe, it didn't give them the best resilience tools. What sometimes seemed to happen was that, quite understandably, people only felt safe if they avoided *all* risk. But good resilience involves judging risk as well as possible and then making informed decisions about how to live our lives.

So, how are we supposed to know what is the best information in other situations?

Here is my advice:

♥ Trust the website or written materials produced by leading charities or government organisations – for example, your country's publicly funded health organisations or best known charities. Even though they might not always get every detail right (because evidence changes), they usually *will* and they have access to the best research.

♥ If you're not sure whether a particular organisation or person is to be trusted, do an internet search for criticism of it. Is there a lot of disagreement from people who sound trustworthy?

♥ Read more than one source.

♥ A book is likely (but not certain) to be more trustworthy than a single article, as long as the book has been published by a reputable publisher rather than self-published. (There's nothing wrong with a self-published book, but you don't have the reassurance of a team of editors and others trying to make sure it's valid and reasonable.) However, remember that the author of a book or an article might still only tell one side of an argument or viewpoint. If in doubt, read something else, too.

- ♥ Go for books or articles that use lots of different research rather than one source.

- ♥ Does the writer seem to be trusted by other sensible people? Do they have a body of books and articles and ways for you to see that they seem to know what they're talking about? For example, someone who has studied a topic for years is more likely to have good information than someone who has just decided to write about their personal experience. Personal experience can be useful but remember that it is just that one person's experience: unless they've also studied the wider picture, they may not have advice that fits *your* situation and experience.

- ♥ Don't trust comments beneath online articles. You have no way of telling whether they are reliable. Mistrust shouting and insults!

KNOW BUT DON'T AVOID YOUR TRIGGERS

Are there certain things that make you especially anxious or distressed? For example, it's quite common to be afraid or wary of:

- ♥ Germs and sickness.
- ♥ Speaking in public; being looked at.
- ♥ Anything to do with death – relating to yourself or others.
- ♥ Spiders, wasps, snakes and various other creatures.
- ♥ Tests and exams.
- ♥ Speaking to strangers or being in groups of people.

Sometimes, these fears start to dominate a person's life, making it hard to do ordinary and important things. They can develop into a phobia – an obsessive fear.

Some people develop fears or phobias about very specific things, including objects which might seem odd to be afraid of, such as cotton wool, pumpkin seeds, banana skins or clowns. (Those are all recognised phobias.)

If there's something you're afraid of, the usual reaction is to try to avoid it. This is very understandable but might not be the best idea. The ideal is that you learn to have an appropriate reaction, rather than a hyper-stressed one.

If you always avoid the things you're afraid of, you never learn to manage the anxiety. The anxiety can start to affect and dominate your life.

Take speaking in public, which is a common thing to fear. Everyone who has spoken in public probably felt very nervous about this at one time. The more you do it and the more you learn to manage your nervousness, the easier it becomes. But if you always avoid the opportunities to do it, you'll never learn to overcome your fear and you'll never experience the pleasure and pride of doing it.

If there is something which you feel you are so afraid of that it's making your life distressing or difficult, you can ask your GP to refer you to a therapist who can help. Don't suffer in silence: there's no need!

RESILIENCE AND TRIGGERS

A trigger warning is when a writer or speaker says that they are about to mention a topic which could trigger distress in some readers, who might have had a traumatic experience. The warning is there to alert the reader so that they can be ready for it or can choose to avoid reading or listening. But are such warnings helpful? Do they improve resilience or hinder it?

Our emotions are triggered by all sorts of events, thoughts and words. If we have had a bad experience, unpleasant memories can be triggered by someone telling a story relating to it, or by a photo or idea or almost anything that brings those memories and emotions flooding back. No one enjoys recalling a horrible memory.

But sometimes it is more than unpleasant: it is deeply distressing and might feel unbearable. In severe cases, where a very bad thing has happened which the person isn't able to deal with, they might be diagnosed with post-traumatic stress disorder (PTSD). This usually requires therapy to help the person move to a better state of mind in which they are able to have the memory without the awful emotions.

In order to lead a full and healthy life, we do need to be able to deal with the things that trigger strong negative emotions. We need, in short, to be resilient.

I have a young relative whose severe obsessive compulsive disorder (OCD) was triggered by anything to do with death. Since it is impossible to go for more than a few days without hearing stories or seeing pictures that remind us of death, or passing graveyards or churches, her symptoms were triggered very often. She could not avoid this so she had to learn – with a great deal of professional help – to become resilient to such triggers.

Some people try to avoid their triggers and I understand why you would want to do that. But it's not possible to live a full life while avoiding common words or ideas, and it's not reasonable to expect everyone else to avoid certain important topics that should be discussed openly so that we have good understanding. And avoiding doesn't make us resilient.

Although trigger warnings have been a popular tool used by caring people to try to help those suffering traumatic memories, more recent research favours not using these warnings. The evidence is that there can be two negative results: first, the person actually experiences more anxiety, not less. And second, they come to see their trauma as the central thing about them, instead of learning to reduce its impact.

Resilience is not about avoidance but finding the strength to face and live with and then overcome our biggest fears. If you can do this yourself, by following the ideas in this book, that's wonderful. But if you have had some really tough experiences or events in your life and you feel vulnerable to certain conversations, words, ideas, stories or topics, you would benefit from talking to someone who is an expert in both your situation and how to help you live your life fully and healthily despite what has happened to you.

Trigger warnings – where a film or book or conversation begins with the warning that certain topics will feature – might seem like a good and caring idea. I used to think so myself. But they turn out not to be effective at building resilience. There may be some exceptions: for example, if you have a very good understanding of your traumatic memory and the trigger warning allows you to take a breath and prepare your mind to cope with confidence, this could be a positive situation.

My suggestion would be as follows. If you are being treated for an anxiety disorder, PTSD or phobia, ask your therapist about trigger warnings. If you're not being treated but you feel there is a topic that upsets you a lot, use your instincts and perhaps discuss with someone who knows you well, before reading a story featuring your triggers. But don't feel you have to avoid these stories: managing your reactions is the aim. Trigger warnings alone just help you avoid things and that is not the best way, even though it might seem attractive at the time.

A WORD ABOUT CRYING

All the above are *deliberate* positive coping strategies, but let me say something about crying, which is usually not deliberate. When we feel really sad about something, having a "good cry", as people sometimes call it, can make us feel better. It's perfectly OK to let out our emotions that way. It is also useful because it is a sign to the people around us that we need comfort and help. It's even possible that this is how crying evolved as a reaction, because the sympathy that people feel for us can be really helpful and bonding. If people didn't cry, others might not know they were feeling sad or in pain or distressed.

Crying a lot, when there's no obvious reason, can also be a sign that we aren't well, alerting us to get help. It's common for someone with depression to find that they often cry at what seem like very small things or even just spontaneously. If this is happening to you, do see your doctor: your body is telling you that something isn't right. It could also be something quite temporary, such as being overtired or fighting off a virus or a delayed reaction to a shock or bad event in your life.

Of course, there are many obvious and very natural reasons why someone might cry a lot, with the most obvious one being grief. Grief can hit us in many different ways and does not have a standard pattern of emotions as some people suggest: if you have gone through the awfulness of losing someone you cared about (or if you are facing that at the moment), don't be surprised at the array of emotions you feel and don't be surprised if you cry more – or less – than you think you should. There is no "should" in grief.

REBUILD YOUR COPING STRATEGIES AFTER A BAD TIME

After you've gone through something bad, your coping strategies may have taken a big knock. You might have used some negative ones or forgotten some positive ones, or just not managed to use them at the right time. You might feel some of them worked and some didn't. What can you do to build them up again?

1. Notice what did help. Make a note in case you need to use these strategies again.

2. Choose a selection of things that worked and think about how you can spend more time doing them. For example, if you found a benefit to going for a long walk or a half hour run, or if you discovered how relaxing a long bath or a breathing exercise could be, think about how you can build these into your week so that they become part of your routine.

3. Acknowledge any negative strategies you used. Don't beat yourself up or feel guilty – everyone makes mistakes – but think about which positive strategies you would use instead next time. If you think you'll need help to do this, ask for it now rather than waiting until something happens again.

4. Sometimes, especially after a really distressing time or event, or if you feel you've moved to a new chapter in your life or development, it can be really helpful to make other changes. These can be quite practical and relatively small things, such as moving all the furniture in your room and having a good clear-out of old clothes and other items; or it could be taking up a new sport or hobby or interest. Go for it! You've come through the

distressing setback in your life and you are a new person, so finding even a small way to show this to yourself can be empowering. You've changed: make that change positive!

REFLECTION ACTIVITY

Go back to page 85 and reread about Naomi, Ollie and Pavel.

Do you think Naomi should carry on with gymnastics competitions? If she does, what advice would you give her? If she doesn't, what advice would you give her?

Can you think of a time when you avoided something that you knew you should do because you were scared or anxious? How did it make you feel? What would have been a better coping strategy, rather than avoidance? Did you manage to learn from your experience?

Do you think Ollie will manage to stick to his positive coping strategies? What would you say to his parents about their negative strategies?

Can you now see positive coping strategies that Naomi, Ollie's parents and Pavel could have used instead of avoiding competition, drinking alcohol, smoking and overusing computer games?

You can see my personal suggestions to these questions on page 181.

SUMMING UP

Coping strategies are the various actions we take to try to reduce or heal mental and emotional distress. If we choose the right strategies, they will act like a protective shell which will make us stronger as we face future difficult events. If we choose the wrong ones, we might feel better at the time but they can make us weaker, less healthy and less able to face challenges later. That's how positive coping strategies increase resilience and negative ones decrease it. Positive ones not only help us immediately but also build our resilience for the future.

Both positive and negative coping strategies quickly become habits, and we want to build good habits that will become part of our daily lives and help us be mentally and physically strong. We shouldn't wait for problems before we start using positive strategies: if we've built the right habits when times are easier, we can quickly carry out healthy actions when our mind is occupied by problems.

TOP TIPS FOR BUILDING POSITIVE COPING STRATEGIES

1. For each challenge you face, think carefully about what would be a healthy coping strategy, one that will not only help in the short term but also in the long term. Try to work this out while you're feeling fairly calm, rather than when you're caught up in strong emotions. If you are overwhelmed by strong emotions, ask someone to help you see things more clearly and analytically.

2. Have a small list of activities that help you in different situations, so that you can easily pick the one you need and use it immediately. Write your list down and keep it where you can quickly find it.

3. Don't suffer in silence. If you feel you can't cope by yourself, there will always be someone able and willing to listen. They might have a solution but, even if they don't, talking almost always helps.

DIARY TIME

Here are some things you could record in your diary, as well as the practical activities:

1. Three things you learnt from this chapter.

2. Each day, if possible, do the "What went well?" activity from page 108.

3. Did you identify or empathise with any of the characters at the start of this chapter?

4. Are there any negative coping strategies you think you have? Would you like to stop using them and, if so, how might you do that? Remember that you might need help, particularly if it's something you've been doing for a while or something that feels very distressing.

5. Write a letter to yourself giving great advice about your worries.

CHAPTER FIVE:
BUILD YOUR COURAGE

HOW DOES THIS HELP RESILIENCE?

A major part of resilience is the courage to keep going, or to try again when it was painful the first time, or to face a challenge that seems too difficult or distressing, rather than running away, avoiding it and believing you can't succeed. But just telling someone (or ourselves) to be brave isn't enough. We have to take active steps to grow our courage.

Resilience involves believing that we can do difficult things and that they won't overwhelm us, and that starts with having the courage to try. And having the courage to fail sometimes, and to learn from those times so that we can succeed next time. Or the next time.

Courage and resilience, therefore, are tightly entwined. Courage comes first; resilience follows; and that, in turn, makes courage easier.

TEENAGE EXAMPLES

Let's see some examples of people having difficulty with courage. I am not judging them: some people have extremely painful things to face and many lack support and encouragement, so they find it much harder to find courage when they need it.

♥♥♥

Roman absolutely hates school. Each morning when he wakes up, his stomach sinks with dread and his heart immediately starts racing. He feels physically sick and his stomach hurts. If he's staying with his dad, his dad usually makes it quite easy for him to stay home. If he's staying with his mum, she usually tries to make him go in, but often she just can't face forcing him so she doesn't. Then he feels relieved but there's also a dark feeling inside. He feels ashamed for being scared but he just can't do anything about it. His mum constantly asks him what he hates so much about school, but the truth is he doesn't really know. It's just full of fear for him: people looking at him, expecting him to behave a certain way, not being sure who his friends are, the difficulty of concentrating all the time, the noise, worrying about being asked a question and not knowing the answer. It doesn't seem sensible to be so scared of such things but he is.

Roman knows that he will have to go to school. But not today. Please, not today. Maybe next week? But the thought makes him feel sick. Maybe he can avoid it until he's old enough to leave?

♥ ♥ ♥

Solomon doesn't hate school, but he does hate a couple of boys in his class who are making his life difficult. They always like someone to pick on and Solomon is now one of their targets. Solomon has always preferred to be quiet in class but recently when he dared answer a question, a girl said, "Oh, wow! He speaks!" And everyone laughed. From then on, the annoying boys have picked on him. Now he wants to stay quiet and never speak up again. He gets good marks on written tests but tries to avoid anything where his voice has to be heard. He now dreads being asked to do anything in front of the class. Everyone laughing at him just confirmed that he's the shy one and should stay that way.

Solomon knows – fears – that one day he'll have to speak in public. The class is taking it in turns to do an assembly on a topic they're passionate about. Solomon hasn't volunteered yet – obviously. Maybe he can avoid it for so long that the term will end or the teacher will forget or a virus outbreak will close the school? He's hoping!

♥ ♥ ♥

Thalia started going to circus school when she was nine. It was a summer holiday treat from her gran and she loved it. Over the next few years she went to classes any time she could and in between she practised acrobatic moves on the trampoline in her garden. One day she landed awkwardly, twisting her knee with excruciating pain. During the three boring months of recovery, Thalia had a big fear: that it would happen again, but worse. Her mind started playing tricks, going over and over imaginary accidents. What if, what if, what if? When she went back to circus school, she couldn't find the courage any more: there was too much fear, too many "what ifs?" Her teacher was kind and reassuring but Thalia couldn't cope with the disappointment: her dreams were over, she thought. She didn't go back the next day.

Thalia really wants to be able to go back to circus school. But what if...? So, maybe she never will.

Roman, Solomon and Thalia are all afraid of something. They didn't choose to feel like this but they haven't (yet) found the courage to do the difficult things they need to do. They feel too negative about what might happen, too worried that it will turn out badly. That negative, pessimistic feeling is making them avoid things that would be likely to improve their lives. They need help and support to find courage. Then they'll find their resilience is stronger and they can face not just the problems they have now but also other hurdles that will challenge them during their lives.

WHAT IS COURAGE?

Not being scared is not the same as having courage! Someone who has no fear doesn't necessarily have courage. Courage means feeling scared but doing something anyway.

But courage also needs to be intelligent and rational. Courage is when you can see that there's a bit of risk but you analyse it carefully, using all the information you can find. You try to balance two things: the risk and the benefit (what you will gain from doing the action). Courage is when you know there's a risk but you decide that you should do the thing anyway and you psych yourself up to do it.

There are many times you'll need courage in your life. You might need it to push you towards auditioning for a role in the school play, or applying for a course or a job. You might need to find courage to speak to someone you're attracted to or to break off a relationship when you know it's not working. You might need to tell your family that you don't want to do the thing they have been hoping you'll do. You might need to stand up for what you believe in or tell an important truth that some people might not like. You might find yourself the victim of bullying or hatred, or you might need to support someone else who is. You might make a big mistake and need to own up to it and apologise or admit that you were wrong. And you might need to face a physical danger.

Courage is what we need when we are scared of something but know it would be better if we did it. We think about the benefits of doing it: maybe we will feel proud, or we will have fun; or the opportunity might lead somewhere; we'll make friends; we'll improve our knowledge or skills. We decide that the possible or likely benefits outweigh the fear.

WHAT ABOUT PHOBIAS?

You know that a phobia is a very strong fear of a particular thing. (I mentioned this on page 118.) Whether a phobia is common, such as a fear of spiders, or rare, such as a fear of pumpkin seeds, it's real to the person suffering it. We often call these fears "irrational" but this doesn't mean you're being silly if you have them. The cause might be obvious or it might be impossible to trace, but when we say "irrational" we mean that the fear response is stronger than it should be and that the rational part of your brain finds it hard to overcome the fear emotion.

Take wasps, for example. (Supposing you aren't allergic to wasps so they're not dangerous to you.) It's rational to be anxious when one settles on your arm or flies behind your head where you can't see it. But if your fear leads you to scream and thrash around, this is irrational because the rational part of your brain should tell you that this will make the wasp angrier, which you obviously don't want. If you have a strong fear or phobia you won't be able (or you'll find it very difficult indeed) to stop yourself screaming and thrashing around. Your heart will be racing and your stress reactions will be high. Wasps produce that response in lots of adults!

So, a phobia is when you cannot control your stress response to a particular thing and you fear it more than is reasonable.

Finding courage when you have a genuine phobia is very difficult indeed. For many people it could be impossible without professional help and therapy.

Roman, in the example at the start of this chapter, has a phobia about school. He feels dread at the thought of it, even though he knows this isn't really rational. If you asked him why he is so afraid, he would only be able to explain in emotional terms: "I hate it. I feel so awful. I feel so scared when I'm there."

Solomon, on the other hand, doesn't have a phobia about school: he is naturally afraid of being teased. Both of them need resilience in the face of their fears so that they can make the most of life's opportunities.

If you have a phobia and especially if it is preventing you from doing things you need or want to do – such as going to school, meeting friends, trying new opportunities, joining in – it would be sensible to get professional help. Tell a trusted adult and they will advise you how to find it.

If you have a phobia, do not blame yourself for not yet having the courage you want: that would be like blaming a toddler for falling over when learning to walk.

SOCIAL ANXIETY

Social anxiety is a type of phobia: a fear of interacting with people. It's common and natural to be a bit nervous about talking to people we don't know well but some people feel this extremely strongly. The anxiety can dominate their lives and make many aspects of normal human interaction really difficult. If you have severe social anxiety, you could need professional help to overcome it, or advice from organisations that support people with this fear. There are some in the Resources section on page 187.

Talking to people we don't know well is a very important skill, so, whether you have social anxiety or you just find it nerve-racking and feel shy, it's definitely worth trying to tackle. You will find it easier the more you practise.

If, like so many people, you feel nervous and awkward talking to people you don't know well, here are my tips for building the courage to overcome this fear:

1. Realise that most people feel some anxiety when talking

to strangers. It's a natural defence mechanism. We worry that they'll laugh at us or that we won't know what to say. It's also normal to feel that people are looking at you and judging you. Accepting this as a normal fear can help you find courage.

2. Realise that to overcome a fear we have to practise. This is a skill like any other and practice does make it easier.

3. Set yourself small targets at first. Don't expect to be able to walk into a room full of strangers and chat easily straightaway; choose a smaller goal, perhaps asking a shop assistant where something is, or someone at a bus stop whether this is the right bus, or making a comment about the food in the lunch queue or asking someone on their own in your class whether they saw a particular TV show.

4. Share your challenge: get someone to support and encourage you. Tell someone that you're trying to be bolder about social interactions and get them to work out small challenges for you. Choose someone who isn't a very socially confident person so that they understand your fears. But most people will empathise with you, because, as I say, it's a common feeling.

5. Practise making eye contact, even if you don't speak. This can be very difficult for some people but you only have to look at someone's eyes for a few seconds at a time. If you find it very difficult to do it at all, just start with two seconds – a mere glance. It will become easier, I promise!

6. Rehearse what you want to say in your head. Sometimes we don't have time to do this but it's often a good idea, especially if we care about saying the right thing. Just don't rehearse it for so long that you lose the right moment to say it! (This happens to me quite often!)

7. Take a few slow, deep breaths as you pluck up the courage

to speak, and one immediately before you open your mouth. When people are about to give a radio interview, they are encouraged to do this, as nervousness can make your voice sound squeaky or breathless and a few extra deep breaths solves this problem.

8. Try to remember that most of the time people are not looking at you, or, if they are, they're only looking at you because it's polite to glance at someone while they're speaking. They are rarely thinking anything in particular. Anyway, some people will like you and some people won't: your job is to do the best you can to be confident in yourself, your value and your right to exist and be heard.

PRACTICAL ACTIVITY

Make a phone call. Talking on the phone can be surprisingly hard, sometimes even harder than face to face, because we don't have the person's body language to tell us when to talk or when to listen. But making phone calls is a useful exercise, even in the days of email and online interaction. So, could you make a phone call today? It could be to someone you know – and you can even tell them in advance you're going to do it and explain why, if you want! It could be to a grandparent, aunt, uncle or other related adult. Or it could be to an organisation or store to ask for information.

Plan how you're going to start the conversation. Plan for how you might have to repeat it because people often don't hear the first few words of a call.

Take a few deep breaths and do it! Find the courage: I know it's there!

POSITIVE STRATEGIES FOR COURAGE

Here are some ways that you can build and practise your courage. See how many of them you can do. Maybe you could choose to do one today?

BE OPTIMISTIC

This chapter was originally going to be called "Build your optimism" but I chose "courage" because that suggests something more active, more deliberate, more self-respecting than simply optimism. Optimism has a sense of "I believe a good thing could happen". Courage feels more like "I can make a good thing happen – I can do this".

Optimism is crossing your fingers and hoping for success; pessimism is closing your eyes and waiting for disaster; courage is gathering all the strength and skills you need for the task. So, courage is better than mere optimism: it gives you more strength, more resilience.

But optimism is a good character strength, too, and worth building. We need to believe that the best result is entirely possible and even likely, rather than assuming the worst. Optimism is also linked to a growth mindset.

How do we build optimism? How do we start to believe that good things can happen to us if that's not what we believe already? Especially if bad things have happened to us before.

Optimism is a good mindset to cultivate. But how? The rest of this chapter gives you strategies to build your optimism and your courage. And therefore your resilience!

PRACTICAL ACTIVITY

Think about yourself. Do you feel you have a generally optimistic nature? Choose which answer describes you best in these scenarios:

1. If I enter a raffle or prize draw:
   a. I find myself thinking, "Oh, imagine if I won – I could..."
   b. I find myself thinking, "I never win these things."

2. If I enter a competition for something I'm reasonably good at:
   a. I imagine myself winning. I visualise receiving a prize.
   b. I don't usually imagine winning. I worry how I'll feel when I don't do well.

3. If a teacher is about to read out the names of students who have been selected for something positive:
   a. I am eagerly expecting that my name will be called out and it doesn't seem surprising if it is.
   b. I do not think it will be me and I am astonished if it is.

4. If I was told that in the next 24 hours I would either come down with flu or something nice would happen:
   a. I would guess it would be something nice.
   b. I would guess it would be flu.

5. I think I'm generally:
   a. A lucky person – good things often happen to me.
   b. An unlucky person – bad things often happen to me.

6. When two bad things happen to me in a row, I'm more likely to think:
   a. Two bits of bad luck – I'd better be more careful!

b. Oh no – accidents happen in threes, don't they?

7. When it's a new school term:
   a. It feels like a fresh start – I will do so much better than before.
   b. I wonder what will go wrong this term.

8. I've heard that it's unlucky to walk under a ladder or break a mirror:
   a. But that's just a superstition and there's no basis in science, so I ignore it.
   b. So I avoid walking under ladders and if I did break a mirror I'd look out for bad luck.

You might have difficulty deciding some of your answers. After all, the situations can vary so much and we all have good and bad days or weeks or even months. And when things are going badly, it's hard to stay positive. But try to step back and answer in a general way, using your imagination and honesty and self-knowledge. If a situation hasn't applied exactly to you, think of something similar.

The more "a" answers you gave, the more optimistic it sounds as though you are in general or you feel at the moment. Six to eight "a" answers suggest that you are strongly optimistic and six to eight "b" answers suggest that you are somewhat pessimistic. Four to five either "a" or "b" answers would put you right in the middle, neither particularly optimistic or pessimistic. This might be because recently some good or bad things have happened to you, though: it might not be how you'll feel if you answered the questions on another occasion. Overall your answers give you a sense of how optimistic or pessimistic you are. And that's useful because it helps you see what to work on.

MAKE YOUR OWN LUCK

You now have an idea whether you are more an optimist than a pessimist. A similar question would be: do you think you're a lucky or unlucky person?

It's hard to deny that some people seem luckier than others. There's luck involved in which adults bring you up and how well they are able to give you all the love that a child needs; and in whether your family has enough money for a comfortable home, food and clothes, as well as for holidays and luxuries. There's luck in the opportunities and experiences you have from the moment you're born. You probably know people who seem to keep having horrible things happen to them.

There is certainly a great deal of luck involved in human lives. Good luck is not something to be proud of (just grateful for) and bad luck is not something to feel ashamed of or blame ourselves for in any way.

But there's research that suggests that there are things we do which can have an effect on some of the things that happen to us.

The psychologist Richard Wiseman has written about this in his book, *The Luck Factor*. He and his researchers carried out lots of studies on the behaviours of people who described themselves as either very lucky or unlucky. The results still don't mean we should blame ourselves if we have bad luck but they do give us some hope that there are actions we could take to give us the chance of finding more positive opportunities.

For example, Wiseman describes how he set up an experiment in which two people, a man who described himself as lucky and a woman who described herself as unlucky, were put in exactly the same situation. How would they behave? Might their behaviours help explain their belief that they were lucky or unlucky?

The experiment was set up identically for each, but at separate times. The man noticed the £5 note left for him to find on the pavement; the woman walked past without seeing it. In the café where Wiseman's researchers had placed actors, the man engaged in conversation with one playing the part of a businessman. The woman didn't talk to anyone. Afterwards, the two of them described their day to the researchers very differently, with the man mentioning finding the money and the interesting conversation he had, and the woman not having anything to report about her day.

Now, this was just two people (other studies involved more) and there are plenty of explanations for why they might have behaved as they did: perhaps the woman was shy, or feeling unwell, or just didn't want to talk, as was entirely her right. Perhaps culturally the woman felt inhibited from talking to strangers, especially a man, and this is why she chose to stay quiet; perhaps she was intensely thinking about something and had no desire to chat to random strangers. Perhaps the man was just on great form that day and everything was going right for him. So, on its own this is not strong or compelling science.

But perhaps this experiment and the others that Wiseman and his colleagues conducted do also suggest some things:

- ♥ That if we are alert we are more likely to see opportunities.
- ♥ That if we are courageous and talk to people (if appropriate) we can get more out of life because you never know what might be sparked by a conversation.
- ♥ That if we wait for doors to open for us, they might not, so we should open them for ourselves.
- ♥ That a positive outlook and an energetic way of approaching the world can bring benefits, create relationships and spark ideas.
- ♥ That "luck" is not always purely random chance: that we can perhaps *sometimes* affect it.

Wiseman talks about "the luck principle", which involves four factors: maximising your opportunities, trusting your intuition, expecting positive events and turning your bad luck into good. I've put a link to a YouTube video explaining this in the Resources section but here are examples of how you might apply these principles in your life:

- ♥ Maximise your opportunities: sign up for that audition; decide to start a new hobby or sport; join a new after-school activity; listen really hard in class.

- ♥ Trust your intuition: decide not to get involved in rule-breaking activity with your friends because you know it's unwise; stay alert while walking outside – you will notice much more, both good things (£5!) and bad things (danger).

- ♥ Expect positive events: when you start a test, believe that you can do well; when you enter a competition, believe that you can win.

- ♥ Turn bad luck into good by finding advantages in every setback: if you hurt yourself, be glad that you didn't hurt yourself more seriously and be grateful for the kindness you receive from others; if you fail a test, know that when you eventually succeed you'll feel even better because you failed at first; if a friendship breaks down, remind yourself that in that case it was going to break down eventually anyway so better that it happens now.

Doing all those things whenever possible will help give you a more optimistic view and the best chance of lucky things happening to you. But remember that, if unlucky things happen, this does not mean that you failed. Understanding that there are things you can do to increase your luck will help you feel optimistic and that will help you find the courage to keep trying.

PRACTICAL ACTIVITY

Next time you go out of your house, spend an hour (or however long you can manage) being observant. If you're on a street or in a public place, see if you can find a coin someone has dropped. But don't only look at the ground: notice people and imagine where they're going and who they are. What kind of lives might they lead? Notice buds on trees, try to spot three different kinds of bird and three different kinds of insect. Find something you can't identify and then, when you get a chance, try to discover what it is. You will be opening your mind to new experiences and that's the first step towards becoming "lucky".

BE REALISTIC

Let me tell you some things you don't want to hear: you can't do everything; you can't be "anything you want to be"; some of your dreams won't come true.

No one can have everything they want, unless they want very little indeed. If you have big dreams, as I hope you do, some of them probably won't come true. If you have big ambitions, as I hope you do, you probably won't succeed at all of them. You might succeed at so many that you don't mind about the ones you miss, though, and that's a brilliant result.

What is most likely is that your life will be a rich mixture of goals you do achieve and goals you don't.

The secret is to aim high, yes, and even to have some dreams, hopes and ambitions that you understand are quite unlikely – although possible if you work hard, learn well and have the luck you need – but to recognise that those dreams might not come to pass. You might "fail".

Resilience is about how you deal with that failure, not how

you avoid failure by only aiming low.

Aim high but don't beat yourself up when you don't make it. Don't kid yourself that everything is possible because then, when you don't achieve *everything*, you'll blame yourself and fail to enjoy and be proud of what you did achieve.

SPOT YOUR LEARNED HELPLESSNESS

Most of our behaviours are "learned". In other words, over time we have learned the behaviour in response to what happens to us when we do it. For example, we learn not to touch something hot because we experience pain when we do; we see (or think about) our favourite sugary treat and we desire it because we've learned that we like the taste and the feeling it gives us in our mouth.

One person might learn to listen carefully in class because they experience benefits from this: the teacher praises them, for example, or they find themselves learning easily. Over time, this behaviour replicates itself in many ways. They become the person who listens and behaves well for the teachers.

Another person, however, might learn to misbehave in class because they have not experienced benefits from listening carefully. Maybe they listen carefully but still don't understand and that feels frustrating. Or perhaps they learn that they get status from their friends if they misbehave.

We learn good and bad behaviours. You might learn to be loving, kind and generous. That's good. But people also learn to bully because they like feeling powerful. They've learned a bad behaviour.

If you think about all the very many things you do or say or think during a day, you'll see how many of them involve decisions based on what you've learned from experience. "When I did that, this happened, so if I do that again, then this is likely, so I will/won't do that." You may not notice yourself thinking this but on some level you are. We do it all the time.

"Learned helplessness" is when someone has had many experiences, usually from a very early age, of not succeeding or not being able to sort out their own problems. Imagine if some or all of these things *often* happened to a child:

- ❤ They are hurt by one or more of the adults who are supposed to care for them.
- ❤ When they need help, they are ignored.
- ❤ They don't experience someone loving them unconditionally.
- ❤ They are very often expected to do things they can't possibly do and told off when they don't.
- ❤ They are criticised or told they're useless, stupid, pathetic, ridiculous.

You can imagine that such a child would not grow up feeling strong and confident about their abilities and potential. They would assume that things would go wrong and they would feel helpless. They would very likely stop trying to succeed at anything because they believe that success isn't possible for them. It would be harder for such a child to be resilient because those negative experiences would weaken them. And it would be more difficult for them to find courage to keep trying through all that negativity and struggle, that experience of being helpless.

There's another group of children who might also find themselves being unconfident and helpless in situations which other children of their age could succeed in:

- ❤ Their parents always do everything for them instead of showing them how they could do it themselves.

♥ Their parents always sort out problems for them.

♥ Their parents protect them from even small dangers so nothing challenging ever happens.

Such parents are often called "helicopter parents". They are so reluctant to let any bad thing happen to their child that they hover and swoop down to sort the problem before it affects them. These children learn that they can't sort things out for themselves. They learn that things just happen to them and they have no power.

If you fall into either of these categories, you might feel vulnerable and have a sense of powerlessness. The message behind this book is that you can learn and that you are capable of so much more than you think. You can become resilient even from such a difficult start.

No one of your age is helpless: you all have power and ability to do things, to take some control. Learning to believe and feel that you are not helpless will start to grow your courage and that will build your resilience.

PRACTICAL ACTIVITY

Think of three things that you can do independently that you couldn't do when you were five or six. Don't just think of school-based things such as maths or history but more general skills. For example, can you go to a friend's house on your own or choose how to spend your free time or find out information online? Can you go to the library or shops? Can you make a phone call?

Now think of things that you can't do independently yet. Write down as many as you can think of. Is there something that you *are allowed to do* but you're nervous about so you don't?

What small steps could you take towards that goal?

What do you think should be your next step towards becoming more independent and responsible for yourself? Can you discuss this with an adult?

ASSESS THE RISK

Humans of all ages are notoriously bad at judging risk properly. We are frightened of things that carry very small risk and yet easily do things that carry more risk. One very obvious example of this is that most people would feel more anxious about getting on a plane than getting in a car, despite the fact that statistically there are more car crashes per mile travelled than air crashes.

Throughout our day we subconsciously – and sometimes consciously – weigh up risk and come to a conclusion. And the conclusion is often wrong.

Different people are also comfortable with different risks and that is more often about personal feelings than actual measurement of risk. I'm more comfortable with the risk of getting flu than the risk of getting a norovirus, because I'm more afraid of vomiting and nausea than I am of having a fever and feeling terrible. But I realise that getting flu is in fact more serious than a norovirus: there are more risks to my health.

What does this have to do with resilience? Lack of resilience is often linked to wrongly assessing risk. We might be unhelpfully afraid of something, perhaps because of having had a bad experience of it before or perhaps because of having an overactive imagination.

So, your resilience in the face of bad things happening or after they've happened will be improved if you can think about risk a bit more rationally and coolly. This is often not easy and if you are a very anxious person it will be harder for you. But not impossible!

PRACTICAL ACTIVITY

In the face of something that you are worried about, follow this process:

1. Ask yourself what is the worst that can happen.

2. Then ask yourself how likely that is. (If you can, find some actual science or statistics about it, but this might not be possible or practical. You could ask some adults what they think.)

3. Ask yourself what is more *likely* to happen.

4. And what is the *best* that could happen.

5. Finally, ask yourself what you can do to make it *more likely that the best will happen*. And do it! If there's nothing you can do to affect the outcome, push it out of your mind.

Once you remind yourself that we are generally poor at judging risk, then you can start to inform yourself what the real risks are and make a more powerful judgement about what you are comfortable with.

The next point builds from this.

LOOK AHEAD SENSIBLY

We can't know what the future holds but we often try to guess. This can mean that we spend a lot of time worrying about things we can't do anything about. Have you ever lain awake at night worrying "What if...?" and then playing out a disastrous story in your mind? It doesn't help you get to sleep.

There are four sensible and useful ways of looking at the future. In my view, we should do them all! They will help us build courage and, therefore, resilience.

1. **Visualise a time when the thing you're worried about will be over.** When we are very anxious about something, we might be overwhelmed by how we feel now. We forget that it will soon be over and that when it is we will feel very different. Sometimes our overwhelming anxiety stops us performing at our best. If so, a useful way of thinking is, "Imagine how I'll feel afterwards if I don't give this my best shot. And how great I'll feel if I do put my fear aside and give it my best shot. How can I make sure that happens?"

2. **Think about likely outcomes and make plans for them.** This is a practical way of thinking. You focus on the things you could do something about, the things that are useful to spend time on. How do you give positive outcomes the best chance and negative ones the least power?

    For example, suppose you have an important exam coming up. You have to pass it in order to join the course you're desperate to do. You might get the grade you need or you might not – your previous results have varied. Imagine success first: what things can you do to make this more likely? What help do you need to ask for? What planning and organisation do you need? How many hours of work do you need to do and when should you start?

    Now imagine that you don't pass (despite doing all those things or possibly because your plans just didn't work out). How will you feel? How will you pull yourself together? Whose help might you need for that? Will you give yourself some time to recover? Would you be able to retake the exam? Is there another way to get to the goal you want? A different exam? A different course?

3. **Visualise what the future will look and feel like if things go well.** Positive visualisation is a technique commonly used in high level sport. The idea is that you can make small improvements to your performance simply by imagining yourself succeeding. They may only be small differences but they could add up to something meaningful. Races can be won by fractions of a second; exams can be passed by one mark.

If it's possible to affect your physical performance – speed, strength, skills – just by the power of positive visualisation, the same is likely to apply to your mental performance. After all, physical and mental activities all start in your brain. Believing that you can't do something could make you hold back, not try your hardest, give up before you need to. So, believing that success is very possible – and reinforcing that by imagining what that will feel like – could make a difference.

For example, imagine it's the day before your basketball team plays a really important match. These are the things you could visualise: what will it feel like if you're winning? You'll feel buzzing, full of energy, your eyes and mind focused on being in the right place at the right time and doing brilliant interceptions. How will it feel when you score or when you take the ball and spin round in a perfect example of the manoeuvre you've been practising?

The more you think like this the more you'll be thinking like an optimist, like someone who believes that good things can happen. You'll feel bold, alert, ready for action, instead of fearful and negative.

4. **Think about how you will feel if things go badly but you cope and come through stronger.** Since you know that things can go wrong, sometimes through no fault of our own and sometimes because we just didn't manage to do our best that day, it's worth preparing for that. It's important not to dwell on possible negatives too much but it is worth giving them a little bit of headspace. If you can think about how you will cope, how you'll move on, you'll be preparing your mind to be resilient.

    For example, think about that same basketball game. Imagine you make a mistake – you lose the ball to an opponent and they go on to score, or you miss a net which you know you should have got. Will you dwell on this and feel embarrassed for a while afterwards, affecting your play negatively, or will you just push the feeling away and move on, focusing on doing everything right from now on? Will you curse yourself or will you be that reassuring voice that says you *can* do it, tells you to focus? And then, when you do that, think how proud you will feel that you were able to put it behind you and not let it drag you down. You will be resilient: bouncing back from that "failure" or setback.

The next chapter is about how to build your future, not just imagine it!

REBUILD YOUR COURAGE AFTER A BAD TIME

As with the other chapters, you've been reading about building courage in advance of possible difficulties and challenges, but how do you rebuild it after you've been hurt? This is not easy because your instinct tells you that it could happen again. But resilience is all about bouncing back, so how can you boost your courage bank?

Try any of these suggestions:

1. Remember: you got through it. You can do it again.

2. Ask yourself: did you cope better or worse than you'd have imagined? What can you learn from this so that you have courage to face it again if necessary? If you keep a diary, write your thoughts down.

3. If this is something that you know you'll have to go through again (for example, exams), how can you prepare yourself better next time? If it's something you hope you won't have to go through again but it's out of your hands (such as a bereavement): a) what did you learn that could help you if you did and b) how can you make sure the fear of it occupies only the amount of headspace you want it to? Do you need help?

4. Allow your emotions to express themselves sometimes and be prepared for that. It's OK to cry or be angry or even laugh. Now see if you can channel that emotion into courage: you came through and you can do it again.

REFLECTION ACTIVITY

On page 126, you read about Roman, Solomon and Thalia. I said, "Roman, Solomon and Thalia are all afraid of something." Can you say what each one is afraid of, deep down? (There may be more than one thing or more than one way of interpreting it.) What would you say to each of them if you could be a wise and positive voice in their heads?

On page 183, you can read my suggested answers.

SUMMING UP

Courage is not about not being afraid: it's about keeping fear in control so that it doesn't stop you doing what you believe is good for you. Courage becomes easier when we believe that a good outcome is possible and when we know what we can do to make it more likely. Courage is also about how we deal with the knowledge that a bad outcome might happen, feeling confident that we will be able to deal with that, pick ourselves up and try again.

You build your courage by trying and practising, as with any other skill. Each time you are brave enough to keep trying, you are bouncing back, getting back up after being knocked down. That's resilience and you're building it every time, making it more likely that you won't be knocked down next time a strong wind blows.

TOP TIPS FOR BUILDING COURAGE

1. Focus on the things you *have* learnt to do in your life. Make a list of them. Include physical skills, schoolwork skills, types of knowledge you've learnt, friends you've made.

2. Remember the principle of growth mindset: we learn by doing and practising; we can learn difficult and complicated things if we take one step at a time; skills and abilities are things we grow.

3. Know that people who have difficult starts in life can still achieve as much as anyone else. Some of them will even be stronger because of what they have suffered.

4. Remember that things are almost never as bad as we imagine and we very often cope better than we could have expected. Remember a thing you coped with and think

how you'd cope even better next time because of what you learnt. All because you are becoming more resilient, stronger, braver.

DIARY TIME

Here are some things you could record in your diary, as well as the practical activities:

1. Three things you learnt from this chapter.

2. Did you identify or empathise with any of the characters at the start of this chapter?

3. Think about a time when you had to be brave. What happened? How did you feel afterwards?

4. Think about a time when you didn't manage to be brave. If you were to face that situation again, how would you act differently?

5. Do you know someone you think is brave? Write about them and why you think they are brave. What could you learn from them?

CHAPTER SIX:
BUILD YOUR FUTURE

HOW DOES THIS HELP RESILIENCE?

Thinking about the future can be scary or exciting or both.
We all need to be able to dream. Sometimes our dreams will
come true and sometimes they won't. Part of being resilient
is being adaptable to what happens, whether that's dreams
not coming true or new doors opening. The new doors might
be right or wrong for us and might be scary to enter. We need
to spot opportunities and judge whether they are doors we
should go through.

What steps can you take for the best chance of your
dreams coming true? How can you grab the right opportunities,
including following paths that might be different from the
one you thought you wanted? When storms slow your progress
or change your direction, how can you stay afloat and keep
sailing on?

An essential part of this is believing that you have and
deserve a positive future. If resilience is about strengthening
ourselves for the future, we have to believe in this future.
Friends, skills, coping strategies and courage – the topics of
the previous chapters – will be most useful to us if we also
believe we have a future to be resilient *for*.

152

TEENAGE EXAMPLES

Look at these two characters and how they see their futures.

• • •

Kesia's family expect her to go into medicine. Both her parents are doctors, her grandfather was a surgeon and her older sister has started medical training. Kesia has been happy to go along with this. But as the time comes closer for her to apply to university or medical school, she is dealing with a major doubt. Is she really suited to a career as a doctor? Is it really what she wants, in her heart? Her mother says she shouldn't worry about it: once she starts, she'll find a branch of medicine she loves. Kesia lies awake worrying. Everything she reads about being a doctor just doesn't seem like her. The things she most loves spending her time on are reading and writing, and recently she's been starting to dream of a career as a writer.

Kesia raises her doubts with her parents and tells them she wants to do a creative writing course. Her mum says, "Oh, Kes, you always used to write wonderful stories but there's no money in it – you need a proper career, not the uncertainty of being a writer. It's way too risky." Kesia tries to argue but whatever she says they have the sensible answer to. It seems as if she has no choice but to pursue medicine as a career.

• • •

Michael has a difficult home life: his dad died when he was a baby and his mum struggles with depression so Michael often has to stay at home to look after her. He can't imagine going to university and his grandparents always talk about him earning a decent living as a plumber, like his father. No one in his family ever went to university so why should he? He's good with his hands and is quick to learn – what more will he need?

But a couple of Michael's teachers have suggested he should try. He's shown leadership on a recent enterprise project and seems to have great business sense. When his head of year suggests he does a business degree, Michael is shocked – a mixture of excited and scared and proud.

"No way! I couldn't do that!" And he gives all sorts of reasons why he shouldn't. But secretly he's thinking, "Could I?" And he becomes more and more excited by the idea.

Kesia is being pushed towards a particular career that her parents have dreamt of for her but which she is starting to realise might not be what she wants or what suits her. Her parents have a narrow outlook, with a particular academic expectation for her. Michael's family have a narrow outlook, too, but it's different from Kesia's parents': they don't have academic expectations for him.

To be resilient, we need to believe that our future is ours to own and that we have many choices that are in our control. We might make mistakes but if we do we can work to put them right. All the earlier chapters have been leading up to this, developing your skills, confidence, coping strategies and courage so that your resilience can let you build a positive future. Kesia and Michael need to find futures that are good for them. They need to have success on their own terms, jobs that suit them and which they can do well in. They need to see doors that are in front of them and maybe have the courage to push those doors open.

How will you give yourself the best chance to build your future in a way that will allow you to achieve what you want to and be resilient when you don't (or don't yet)?

HAVE A PURPOSE

Having a purpose doesn't need to mean having a long-term goal or destination, because it's absolutely fine if you don't know what you want to be. Having a purpose can be any or all of the things you want to achieve, whether this minute or today or this week or term or further ahead. It can be small things and big things. Having a purpose doesn't have to be rigid and single-minded; it doesn't have to be strict; it can be vague and general; it can be small or huge. It can be anything that moves you forward in a direction you want to go – or several directions at once. Having a purpose just means doing some things deliberately instead of everything by accident or waiting for things to happen to you.

You don't always have to be thinking of your purpose: that would be impossible, and exhausting to try! We do lots of things without thinking about why. Sometimes you'll do things spontaneously or accidentally and the results will be great.

But it is also very helpful to feel a sense of purpose. Most of us feel better when we sense that what we're doing has meaning. In fact, it's often when we think we have no meaning that we feel at our worst, our weakest and most vulnerable. It's when we feel we don't have purpose or meaning that we have less resilience.

You might be wondering how you can find a purpose in your life. So, let's think about opportunities or situations, small or big, when you can build purpose into your life. You'll find it's easier than you might have thought!

THE SKILLS OR KNOWLEDGE YOU WANT

If you love learning anything, you might find this easy but often we don't know where to start. Or often people say things like "I'd love to be able to sing better" but they don't do anything about it. So it could be a good idea to think a little more constructively.

💛 Think about whether you'd like to improve your skills in sport or art or music – which actions today will move you in that direction?

- ❤ Is there something you'd like to know a lot about? If so, what can you do to achieve that?

- ❤ Do you have ambitions to be better at reading, writing, maths, history, science or any specific subjects that you enjoy more than others? If so, this can motivate you to listen better in these lessons.

- ❤ Do you like the idea of certain careers or jobs? You don't have to commit to that path now, but what do you think are the school subjects or out-of-school activities that might fit with those? Are there some choices you could make to move in that direction?

THE PERSON YOU WANT TO BE

I don't want you to fundamentally change who you are, because who you are is important and valuable. But there are probably bits of who you are that you would like to polish and others that you'd like to restrain a little. Are there some behaviours or habits that you feel could be holding you back from where you'd like to be? And some that you're proud of? Here are some ideas to help you:

- ❤ What are your best character strengths? (See page 77.) Pick one or two and write down three things you could do this week that would boost them further.

- ❤ Which do you think are your weaker character aspects? Pick one or two and write down something you could do each day to build them up.

- ❤ Imagining yourself in the future, which of these do you see yourself doing (you can choose several):

    - ⚡ Working in an office as part of a team?

- Working in an office, leading a team?
- Working for yourself and working at home?
- Working outdoors – on your own or with other people?
- Working with numbers or words?
- Being visually creative – e.g. design or art?
- Making things?
- A job which isn't very important to you but which earns you an income?
- A job which is really important to you and makes you want to work long hours?
- Running your own business (and employing other people), with all the risk but all the satisfaction?
- With lots of people around you or not or a mixture?
- A job with lots of stress or definitely not?

What should you do with your answers? Just bear them in mind as you make choices about activities and subjects you take, and where you direct your energy. But keep an open mind, too.

YOUR HEALTHY BODY

Your health is important in your future and it's important now. Eating, exercising, sleeping and looking after yourself will have long-term effects and immediate effects. It's easier to focus on the immediate and short-term effects because we tend to respond more strongly to things when we notice the effects straightaway rather than having to wait a long time for them. So, even though I'm encouraging you to build your future, doing the right things *now* is the right way to do that because what you do now will affect your future. Here are some ways to make sure you're doing this:

💜 Do you have a varied, healthy diet? We need plenty of nourishing food: enough *quantity* to keep our brain and body fuelled and strong, and enough *variety* to ensure we're getting all the nutrients for our skin, nails, hair, eyes, brain, bones, blood and every cell in our body.

💜 Do you have a positive attitude to food? As you know, many people don't: people of all ages can have a negative relationship with food, sometimes eating more than is healthy and sometimes eating far too little. Some people see food as an enemy, something to be controlled or something that controls them, and they often feel very guilty or anxious around food. There are many reasons for this, including eating disorders, which are illnesses that need medical treatment. Eating disorders can become very serious and even fatal so, if you think you have a problem with how you think about food and your body, please get medical help. A cure is much more likely if the problem is caught early.

💜 Are your bones and muscles strong so that you can be physically fit and not be injured unnecessarily? I talked about exercise on page 104 so you know that regular varied physical activity is really important to the health of both body and mind. In terms of your future, the work you put in now will make a difference to the strength of your body in your adult years and to your chances of avoiding some health problems.

💜 Do you usually sleep well? (It's natural to have bad nights sometimes.) If you feel you need to improve your sleep, check out the advice on page 99 and you will find resources at the back of the book. Good sleep habits will help throughout your life.

💜 Looking to your future, your overall health and fitness will help you achieve your goals, partly because you'll have less time off sick. However, don't be anxious if you do often have minor illnesses such as coughs and colds or stomach upsets: it's more common for young people to have such illnesses and you are in close contact with lots of people, making you more likely to catch something. It does not mean that you'll often be ill as an adult.

● You can improve your hair, skin and nails by taking simple healthy steps. A good diet and exercise habit is a great start, but also think about drinking enough water, avoiding too much sugar and having a good hygiene routine. Many people need a bit of extra help to deal with acne or problems with weak and splitting nails. You will find the most reliable advice on medical websites rather than sites trying to sell you expensive products. Your hair, skin and nails will naturally change over the years and many problems disappear by themselves, but the habit of looking after yourself physically is a good one for your whole life.

YOUR HEALTHY MIND

Don't expect to live your life with no worries and no difficult times. Those periods happen to everyone. And this book is about having the resilience to bounce back from them rather than finding ways to avoid them (which would be impossible). Here are some tips for having a healthy mind in the future:

● Believe that you will grow mentally stronger as you get older and that each difficulty that comes along has the potential to help you do just that.

● Expect good things to happen to you, but know that if bad things happen you can deal with them. Don't dwell on worries: allow them to be at the back of your mind and realise that occasionally they will break out and dominate your thoughts for a while. Then send those thoughts packing and get on with your life.

- ♥ Believe that when something you've been worrying about happens, you will cope with it better than you feared.

- ♥ Remember that if every day and every week brought only good things, you would stop appreciating them; they would become ordinary. You might even feel guilty that you were so much luckier than everyone else. Value challenge!

THE SORT OF DAY OR WEEK YOU PLAN

Your future is made of minutes, days, weeks, years and decades. Your long-term future is partly built on all the things – small and big – that will happen in your short-term future. The short-term things are usually the ones that are easier to control and each one is a step along the way. Try to remember that it doesn't matter when you make little mistakes. Here are some ways to think about this:

- ♥ What are your plans and hopes for today? What do you want to achieve? Write down some specific things – such as, "Learn the material for my biology test" or "Eat two sorts of salad with my lunch" or "Ask Mr Pride for help with fractions". You can also write down more general ones, such as "Listen more carefully in class", as long as you write some details about how you will do that. For example, "When Mrs Brace tells us our homework, I will concentrate hard and write it down."

- ♥ What are your plans and hopes for the week? Perhaps you will walk to school every day instead of taking the bus; or you'll make progress with music, art, sport, or whatever you value.

- ♥ Look back at your aims under "The skills or knowledge you want" and "The person you want to be" and see what you could do this week to push one of those forward. The gain might be so small you can hardly detect it and that's fine: this is one day or week out of many!

THE SORT OF MONTH OR TERM YOU WANT TO HAVE

A school term is a decently long time to make change, and yet not so long that the end looks impossible. Here are some ways of thinking about it:

- ♥ Did you have a school report last term? Was there something in it that you'd love to change this term? Can you think of one or maybe two practical actions you could take that would help that happen? You might want to discuss this with a friend or an adult. Keep your ideas sharply focused. For example, "Go to bed at 9.30 p.m. each school night" is better than "Go to bed earlier"; "Switch my phone off while I'm doing homework" is better than "Use my phone less".

- ♥ When you make a mistake or something goes wrong, examine why that happened and see what you could do to stop it recurring. Again, you might like to discuss this with someone.

- ♥ If the changes you want to make are too difficult and you keep having setbacks and no successes, ask for help from a trusted adult. You may be setting yourself targets that are too high or simply not seeing an obvious trigger for things going wrong.

- ♥ Remember to acknowledge and record the things that have gone right. Write them down and remind yourself. Each one of those steps forward is worth building on.

KEEP YOUR OPTIONS OPEN

If you have a very strong and fixed idea of what you want to be, that's fine if it all works out, but what if it doesn't? If you *also* keep other options open by building a wide range of skills, you'll be able to bounce back better if something gets in the way of that strong dream you had. Most school students don't have a fixed idea of what they want to be so schools tend to encourage you to build a wide range of skills and interests, which is excellent. Do take as many opportunities as you can.

Another problem with only having one fixed goal is that it can blind you to an even better opportunity that might appear. Your interests will likely change over time: for example, you might currently think gardening is really boring but suddenly find a passion for it later; you might think you'd hate teaching but in five years' time it becomes something you'd love to do; working in a shop might appeal now but you might change your mind when you get to your next stage of life.

Two thoughts for you:

1. If you *do* have a strong feeling that you'd like to follow a particular career, follow that goal but keep your options open. Don't close doors unless you have to.
2. If you don't know what you want to do, don't worry about this and do keep your options as wide as possible. Don't close doors.

Either way, in other words, keep your options open! It will help you be more resilient to changes in your circumstances, skills, desires and interests as you grow older.

BE AMBITIOUS BUT REALISTIC

Now that you've learnt about building optimism and you know

the importance of a growth mindset, you can be ambitious and realistic at the same time.

You know, for example, that it's no good having an ambition to be a concert pianist if you don't work extremely hard at your piano playing; or an Olympic medallist if you don't put in countless hours of training.

There are lots of possible ambitions you might have for your adult life. Here are some. Which ones do you identify with strongly?

- ♥ To have a very exciting, adventurous life.
- ♥ To have a peaceful life, perhaps in the countryside.
- ♥ To have a buzzing city life.
- ♥ To have a secure job which pays reasonably but brings no stress.
- ♥ To be a boss in a high-profile, demanding job.
- ♥ To start a business on my own and keep it small but interesting.
- ♥ To start a business which becomes big and successful, employing lots of people.
- ♥ To be successful in a creative career – writer, artist, musician etc.
- ♥ To work in a caring role.
- ♥ To be famous.
- ♥ To be rich in any way possible.
- ♥ To have a partner who shares my interests.
- ♥ To have a big family.
- ♥ To be a good person.
- ♥ To work for or support an important cause or charity.

You might think of some others.

Realism comes when you think about the next two questions:

1. In what way do you think those ambitions would suit you?
2. What are the steps you'll need to take to make them more likely to be achievable?

In your teenage years, you may think there's nothing you can do to make achieving those ambitions more likely, and in some cases you'd be right. But it's still worth thinking about what makes you tick, what makes you happy, what you want in life. Those wishes may well change, too, and that's fine because you do *not* have to know what you want to be now.

Being realistic means understanding the steps you need to take in order to achieve something and pushing yourself gently in that direction when the opportunity arises. It also means changing direction when needed, being flexible, not fixed in your thinking.

Being realistic also means accepting that the thing we wish for *might not* happen. I always wanted to be a published author. For twenty years, that didn't happen, much as I tried. (And I was definitely trying very hard.) That was difficult and sometimes demoralising, but I kept myself going by having other ambitions, too, so I didn't only have that one goal. The reasons I eventually achieved my big ambition are:

- ❤ I really wanted it so I kept trying.
- ❤ I kept learning and taking the necessary steps to becoming published (including finding out as much as I could about what those steps were, and getting better at writing and at listening to readers).
- ❤ I was lucky.

The fact that luck comes into whether we achieve our ambitions should never put you off. Success is not *only* about hard work, skills and perseverance: there's also a major element of luck. We need to be realistic about that. It's actually helpful to remember, too, because it stops us totally blaming ourselves. Eddie Jaku, the man whose story I told on page 22, needed luck as well as determination to survive and then achieve his ambition to be happy. It doesn't take away from his achievement.

Resilience to the various setbacks that might get in the way of our ambitions is easier when we are realistic. Sometimes we can't have what we want but, if we set realistic ambitions and work out the steps we need to take, we are more likely to achieve success and also more able to pick ourselves up and try again when things go wrong. We can say to ourselves, "Well, sometimes things go wrong. Time to reassess. Is there another way, or another goal?"

REMEMBER GROWTH MINDSET

Growth mindset seems to make an appearance often in this book! That's because the belief that we improve at everything we do each time we try to do it is so empowering. It's encouraging to know that each attempt we make at something, even if we don't succeed, is still building or strengthening physical neural connections in our brain, changing them positively, usefully.

So, as you think about your future – remembering that you don't need to have a crystal-clear vision of that future – growth mindset will help you to remember that one step at a time you can move towards your goals and give yourself the best chance of achieving them. The knowledge that nothing is guaranteed doesn't take away from that: it just reminds you to keep trying, keep learning, practising, listening, working hard and asking for help when needed.

Growth mindset is fundamental to resilience.

KNOW YOUR "HEARTSONG"

I have left this for last because I think it's the most important thing. Maybe I'm saying this because it helped me so much but I hope it will also inspire you. Here's what it is.

A very wise person – a doctor and counsellor who used his scientific knowledge, common sense and human intuition – once told me that I needed to know what gave me heartsong and make sure I introduced enough of it into my life.

Heartsong is a feeling of joy, of satisfaction, of fulfilment, of happiness. It's different from well-being. Well-being is long-lasting, a background state of health and strength. Heartsong can last a few moments or minutes (or sometimes longer) but it's positive emotion that is just for you, not for anyone else. (Many people get their heartsong from helping others, of course.) It's what makes your heart sing.

Heartsong isn't just the chemicals your brain produces when happy: it's also the feeling of pride or gratitude or delight; it's the thoughts that come to you: "I'm glad I did that", "I enjoy doing this", "This is me".

We all get our heartsong from different things and those things might (and probably will) change as we move through different stages of life.

You can get heartsong from small or big things. Here are some ideas but you will be able to think of different ones:

- ❤ Playing a musical instrument and not making a mistake.
- ❤ Writing a story that everyone listens to and some people cry about.

- ♥ Standing on stage and making the audience feel whatever emotion you intend.
- ♥ Making a speech and having people applaud.
- ♥ Baking a beautiful cake.
- ♥ Winning the lottery.
- ♥ Someone you're attracted to smiling at you or complimenting you.
- ♥ Finishing all your work on Friday and having a whole weekend free.
- ♥ Being selected for a team.
- ♥ Getting full marks on a test.
- ♥ Playing with your dog.
- ♥ Being pleased with a drawing you've done.
- ♥ Singing with a group of people.
- ♥ Watching your team or country win a match.
- ♥ Being praised.
- ♥ Raising money for a charity you support.
- ♥ Having your favourite meal for your birthday, because someone made that effort for you.
- ♥ Anything you're proud of finishing and achieving: making something that's taken you time, skill and effort.

A useful thing I've learnt is that there's big heartsong and little heartsong. Ideally, you'll have several different things that give you this feeling, because sometimes you won't be able to achieve the big things – or at least not yet – so you need the smaller ones to keep you going.

In my case, I knew that my biggest heartsong would come from having books published. Each time I failed, I had to find resilience, so that I could pick myself up and try again. The wise person who told me about heartsong pointed out that I also needed to notice the same feeling from other things: for example, my family, my garden, my creative hobbies, as well as the shorter things that I was having published. Each one, however small or big, was important and would have more effect if I *noticed it*.

The point is that you need to know and notice the things that give you heartsong and give you a positive feeling about yourself and your life. They may each only last a few moments but you can make them last longer by identifying them and valuing them.

A practical strategy for this is the "What went well" exercise from page 108, because that helps you generate a positive feeling, a feeling of gratitude.

WHAT DOES HEARTSONG HAVE TO DO WITH YOUR FUTURE?

When you feel heartsong from something you have done, it gives your confidence a boost. When you see the present in a positive light, it is easier to see your future in a more positive light. You will see yourself as able to do things to affect it. We get heartsong from being successful at things, those positive moments of affirmation, the belief that we matter, that there's a reason for us to keep being who we are and trying to be better than we are now. And if we can create for ourselves a future that contains enough heartsong, we can feel fulfilled and be useful members of society, whatever area of life we find ourselves in, both in our personal lives and in our interactions with people we come across.

WHAT DOES HEARTSONG HAVE TO DO WITH RESILIENCE?

Resilience is not just about picking ourselves up after setbacks and problems: it's much more positive than that. Resilience is also about finding joy in life, building ourselves up with so many affirming, useful, healthy thoughts, feelings and moments that we have enough positive energy from the good times to keep on battling through the tough times. Life is not just about being ready for difficult things: it's also about enjoying the top of the mountain when we get there. In fact, not just the top of the mountain but also the view the whole way up. Don't just keep your sights on the top; don't forget to stop often and marvel at how far you've come. You need those moments of joy and heartsong so you can remember what our lives are for: living.

REBUILD YOUR FUTURE AFTER A BAD TIME

When you've just had a knockback, it can be hard to think positively about your future. Here are suggestions to help you:

1. Sometimes, you don't need to look at the future straightaway. If you don't want to because it seems too hard, that's fine for a while, because being in the present moment is also valuable. If you give yourself breathing space, time to heal a little, you'll soon find the strength to get up and try again – or try something different.

2. It's OK to change direction. That's not giving up but being flexible, open-minded, adaptable. But perhaps you could talk to someone who knows you well before you make any big decisions.

3. Work out what things are really important to you – what makes you you – and stay true to those things.

REFLECTION ACTIVITY

Look back at page 153 and reread about Kesia and Michael.
Think about these questions: do you think Kesia will apply
to study medicine and Michael will apply to university? What
would you tell each of them about heartsong? What other
advice would you give them about their futures?

My own suggestions are on page 185.

SUMMING UP

You do not need to know what you want to "be" and what jobs
your future holds. By keeping your options wide and your mind
open, by knowing yourself and your needs and personality, by
grasping opportunities and by keeping your eyes both on the
horizon and on the steps you are taking now, you can help
shape your future and be ready for all the opportunities that
will come your way. Optimism and realism, self-awareness, a
positive purpose and staying true to yourself and what gives
you heartsong will all help you shape that future and enjoy it
as it unfolds. When the things you plan and aim for work out,
that's very rewarding, but there will also be opportunities that
you don't expect: look out for them and let them take your
future in exciting directions. That way, you'll be resilient to all
your future storms; you'll swim, not sink.

TOP TIPS FOR BUILDING YOUR FUTURE

1. Know yourself. Notice your personality traits, the things that make you happy or sad or inspired or angry, the things that interest you – feed those interests and personal feelings. Your future needs to suit you, not anyone else.

2. Take opportunities and try new things. The more different things you try, the more chances of positive events that could shape your future: meeting someone who changes your life, trying a hobby which leads to a new passion or skills or job, having a conversation which leads to a new enterprise or knowledge about yourself, making a friend who could be really positive for your confidence.

3. If you look far into the future and try to plan, keep those plans wide and flexible. Imagine walking into your future with your eyes and arms wide, trying not to miss any opportunities.

4. When opportunities are lost, let them go. Don't dwell on "if only".

DIARY TIME

Here are some things you could record in your diary, as well as the practical activities:

1. Three things you learnt from this chapter.

2. How would your best friend, most supportive teacher or caring adult describe you honestly? Write down lots of words or phrases to describe you, your personality and your strengths and likes.

3. What might hold you back from the future you'd like? Pick one or two of them and think about how you'll stop that happening. And how you can plan for it in case it happens.

4. Write a letter to your future self from your teenage self.

5. Write a letter from your imaginary future self to yourself now.

For your interest, here is my letter, written aged 59 to how I remember myself aged 15.

Dear Nicola,

I'm really sorry I judged you so negatively and didn't look after you. I didn't understand that you weren't the only person who was full of self-doubts and self-consciousness – most of us were, and certainly the kind, decent, sensitive ones. I didn't understand that although you were doing well at school it wasn't enough to give you confidence, because you were focusing so much on the times you didn't do well and not valuing the times you succeeded. You worked too hard, drove yourself too hard, expected too much of yourself. Let me tell you now that it isn't a good idea to get up so early and work late at night during exams: you'd have done better if you'd looked after yourself and taken breaks.

You think you aren't resilient; you say you're weak. Yes, you've got your weaknesses, like everyone: you don't join in, you focus on failures more than successes, you're incredibly self-conscious and you often avoid competition because you fear failure or messing up in public. You're a perfectionist and you think nothing you do is good enough.

But why not think of the difficult things you did cope with: being the only girl in a boys' school, being the youngest in your class, being left out so often because you were different from your peer group? And all the normal struggles of teenage years and exams and relationships – you got through! You might have felt you were being knocked over but if you were you always got up. And look where you are now! Giving advice to teenagers just like you.

I think you'll get stronger and stronger each year that goes by, each problem you deal with, each time you bounce back again. Not long ago, you had a personal tragedy, an awful loss you never expected. It's not a test anyone would want but here you still are. Stronger still, more resilient. Wiser. A better person?

I think all of us are a bit more resilient than we think and, if we can just give ourselves credit for what we've done rather than what we've not done, we can turn that little seed of resilience into something bigger and stronger.

So, stop beating yourself up and doing yourself down. Be just the right amount of angry or sad or anxious or fearful and turn it into the courage to stay standing or to get up again when you've fallen. Be confident in yourself even when you feel afraid. Keep trying, keep learning, keep growing. Be brilliantly resilient.

With love,
Nicola

FINALLY...

You now have the tools for building your resilience. You can sail across the ocean of your life and weather any storms. You can also enjoy the calm waters and beautiful days along the way.

You've started to become more confident and you know how to focus on developing the skills you want. Your growth mindset helps you remember that when you want to learn something or be better at anything, you can do that by practising, trying, building the connections in your brain that bring success. And you're prioritising your well-being, making sure you eat great food, exercise, sleep well and relax often.

You have some powerful coping strategies and you know how to avoid the harmful ones. You have a whole range of stress-busting solutions so that you can let stress do its job of pushing you to super-performance instead of dragging you down and making you feel awful.

You have grown your courage, finding ways to face the things you fear and to keep those fears in perspective. Bad things happen but the fear of them will not spoil your life, because you won't let it. You can have dreams but those dreams don't have to be exact or planned: you can't know what lies ahead in your future. You do know that there are steps you can take to help push your future in the directions you want and to give you a fulfilling life. Your future may be different from – and better than – how you imagine, and you know how to face it with hope and optimism and courage. That's resilience.

You are far more resilient than you were at the start of this book. You have the tools to become even more so as you go through life, whatever happens to you. It's your future, your life. Be bold, be confident, be proud. Hope and believe. Learn and grow. Be brilliantly resilient. You can do this.

APPENDIX

At the end of each chapter, I asked you to reread about the fictional characters and then think of your answers to some questions. Different people might have different and yet equally valid answers, but here's what I think. See whether you think the same. If you didn't and you had some very different answers, you might like to discuss with friends and teachers.

CHAPTER TWO: BUILD YOUR SUPPORT NETWORK

What do you think Abbie's problems are? What could she do about them? Is she making some mistakes in her thinking? Have you got some suggestions for her? Who might she talk to? Do you think she should talk to Bilal about how she feels?

There are two main problems for Abbie: she lacks friends (which makes her feel like an outsider) and she has become very anxious about everything. What I believe Abbie doesn't realise is that there are lots of other people feeling the same as her, including perhaps those students she sees in the library at lunchtime. I also wish she could see that she has lots of strengths – she sounds very creative and being a quiet person can help her with that, as she enjoys quietly practising her drawing and writing. She needs friends who share her interests and, if she could just try, she'd certainly find them.

So, I would encourage Abbie not to try to change who she is – a sensitive, aware, creative and artistic person who many people would love as a friend – and instead try to find the courage to join an activity that she's interested in, and also to try speaking to people who might share her interests.

She can talk to the school librarian about this. I would also love her to tell her parents that this is how she feels and to ask them to help her do what she knows she needs to: value herself and push herself to join in a little bit more with activities she might like. And, if she wants to, she can talk to any of the other students who seem not to be part of any of the noisy groups. The girl who asked her back to her house, for example. Abbie could think how the girl felt when she'd plucked up courage to invite Abbie and then Abbie said no. Abbie has the power to put that right!

If she can do this her general anxiety should soon fade to a manageable level. Often, feeling alone – whether in our head or in our lives, or both – is a major trigger for anxious thoughts. If Abbie can find connections, she should feel better.

As to whether she should talk to Bilal about how she feels: there's no need. What would she gain? You can't force someone to be friends with you. He did what he needed to do at the time and perhaps their friendship came to a natural end.

What do you think about Bilal and how he and Abbie stopped being friends? Is there anything they should have done differently?

We don't really know enough detail to make judgements here but it's very possible that these friends just naturally grew apart. If Bilal was drawn towards new friends and they shared his interests more than Abbie, there's no reason why he should spend lots of time with Abbie if he doesn't want to. If he only stopped being her friend because his other friends teased him, that's a shame, but I'm guessing it was more than that: they just grew apart. If so, it's neither Abbie's fault nor Bilal's and they would have stopped being friends at some point. Friendships change and fade. Bilal needs his support network too, and if he enjoys being with his new friends and they're good for him then he doesn't need to feel bad, as long as he wasn't mean to Abbie. Maybe when they're a bit older they can be friends again, if they both want that.

What are Chris's main problems? Who could be his support network? Who could he talk to? If you were Chris's friend, what would you say to him? What should he do about his brother? Do you think Chris will be OK?

Chris has a lot to deal with and it's hardly surprising that everything is spiralling downwards and feeling so stressful. He's just had a bad day at school with a bad test result, and he's started to worry that this is going to happen again. His mum and stepdad are preoccupied (and Chris is probably worried about his mum and maybe also about the big change that is coming with a new baby arriving) and his older brother is putting really unfair pressure on him. His stepdad is not close to him and Chris might feel conflicting emotions about his mother's new marriage.

Chris has a potentially really good support network but at the moment he feels he can't access it because a) his mum is preoccupied and he's not close to his stepdad, b) his teachers don't know the stress he's under and c) nor do his friends. Chris can't change the fact that his parents are preoccupied but if he needs them he should be able to ask them for help – just a chat so they know how he feels. But his teachers and his friends are the easiest people to open up to right now and he can talk to his parents later.

If the teachers knew what Chris was dealing with, they would be very sympathetic. I would strongly ask Chris to share his problems with a teacher that he trusts. Or any trusted adult – perhaps his grandparents – could help.

He also has two good school-friends. They don't know he needs them. He could open up to them: I'm confident they'd be on his side.

If I was Chris's friend, I would say something like this: "Chris, it's totally understandable that you did badly in that test! It happens to everyone when they have things on their mind – and you have such a lot to worry about. No one can concentrate and do their best then. It must be really difficult at home and you must be worried about your mum. You need to tell a teacher that things are tough at home and you've got some big worries. You don't have to tell them about your brother – you've got your own worries and he is not your responsibility."

Chris's brother's behaviour is not Chris's responsibility, and perhaps he could tell his brother that he won't stick up for him any more and that he shouldn't drag him into whatever he's doing. If I were Chris, I'd probably talk to my friends about this. They will know the situation better than anyone.

Chris is a hard-working, high-achieving boy: he should not have to doubt his abilities. He can come through this with the help of his support network.

Who should help Seema get the treatment she needs? Do you think her friends are jealous? What do you think her friends should do to help her? Does she have a good support network?

Seema needs professional help and that is the responsibility of the adults in her life. The adults need to access medical help.

Seema's friends are genuinely worried; she thinks they're jealous but I don't think so. Yes, perhaps they too would like their bodies to be different, and wanting to be thinner is unfortunately a common desire in our modern world where we are bombarded by manipulated images of unrealistic body shapes, but they care about her and don't want her to be ill.

The best way for her friends to help her (and each other) is to avoid all comments on weight or looks – even compliments. "You look great" might be interpreted as "You've put on weight – wonderful!" or "You look so slim!", both of which are triggering for people obsessively trying to lose weight.

Seema's friends should avoid discussing calories or fat

content or making any guilt-laden remarks such as, "I wish I hadn't eaten that third cookie."

It can be helpful to say things like, "An eating disorder is a real illness. It's not your fault", "We love you and are here for you", "Our bodies are brilliant because they give us life". And they can find distracting things to do with Seema – sharing favourite books, watching films, developing hobbies. But friends are not responsible for her cure: that's the job of professionals, with support from the adults in Seema's life.

All of us, along with Seema and her friends, should try to think of our bodies as the strong vessels of our life, our power and our potential, not something to be forced into an artificial shape set by advertisers and manufacturers.

Yes, Seema has a good support network but she's suffering from an eating disorder, which is an illness that twists your thinking, so she doesn't recognise the help those people can be.

CHAPTER THREE: BUILD YOUR SKILLS

I asked you to look back at page 61 and remind yourself about Eddie, Fardin, Sadia and Mattie. Do you identify with any of them in some ways? Now that you understand more about confidence and the importance of building skills, what advice would you give each of them so that they can be more resilient to failure or difficulty? Is there one thing you would say to yourself or one thing you will do differently to help you build your own skills?

I personally identify most strongly with Eddie, although I didn't experience my parents splitting up. Like him, I'm the oldest of three and was always used to finding things easy and often coming top. But there were some years at school when I found the work much harder and had bad reports. I started school unusually young – for the first few years I was three years younger than the average age of my class. I was easily the youngest in my year but I didn't make allowances for that, just wondered why, if I was as clever as I kept being told, I couldn't always get high marks. I also avoided the things I was weaker at, as Fardin does. But I didn't know anything about my brain in those days and I didn't realise that we can improve by listening, trying and practising – and being determined!

This is the advice I'd give them all: however "clever" you are told you are, the most important thing is to know that you can become better at anything and find anything easier by practising in the right way, guided by a good teacher (and your parents and other adults can also be that "teacher", as Mattie's dad was). I would say to them that confidence comes from learning skills and acknowledging what you've learnt and how far you've come, because when you notice what you've achieved and how you've changed, you see that you can do even more, step by step. I would encourage them all to notice when they have achieved or succeeded even in small ways, because each success can be built on. And I'd urge them to view any "failure" as an opportunity to learn and improve and grow.

When they hear all that, they will have confidence that they can overcome things that seem difficult. And that is brilliant resilience.

CHAPTER FOUR: BUILD YOUR POSITIVE COPING STRATEGIES

Do you think Naomi should carry on with gymnastics competitions? If she does, what advice would you give her? If she doesn't, what advice would you give her?

I think Naomi should try to look ahead and decide whether she would like to overcome her current lack of confidence at gymnastics. Perhaps in her heart she's feeling that she doesn't love it as much as she did? Will she regret it if she stops completely? She might – but she might not. So I'd advise her to think about this, because there's no point in spending so many hours and so much energy if she would be happier and more fulfilled doing something else. Or perhaps she'd be happier just doing gymnastics for the exercise and fun but taking a break from competitions? I'd advise her to discuss it with her coach and parents and friends and take her time. There's no rush!

If Naomi decides to carry on, I'd suggest she gets some help with her pre-competition nerves. She needs to realise that, although anxiety doesn't feel nice, a certain amount of it will help her perform well, and that there are things she can do to keep the levels bearable and useful. It will also help her if she can look ahead and think how great she'll feel afterwards. If she does decide to stop, I'd suggest she finds something else fulfilling to take its place.

Can you think of a time when you avoided something that you knew you should do because you were scared or anxious? How did it make you feel? What would have been a better coping strategy, rather than avoidance? Did you manage to learn from your experience?

I used to be a keen horse rider but when I was about twelve I had some experiences just like Naomi: every time there was a competition, I'd get a sore throat or headache and avoid going. I felt pretty bad about this, even though they were genuine sore throats and headaches. I knew I was missing out. However, I was never going to be a champion rider and I really did (still do) hate competitions so I stopped entering them. It was probably the right thing to do in practical terms but it didn't build my resilience: sometimes we do need to face a competitive situation, which I'm still very bad at. I don't think I learnt from this experience, I'm afraid! I think I needed a way to build my confidence and courage. Perhaps to talk to someone about why I was running away. But in those days we understood less about how minds work.

Do you think Ollie will manage to stick to his positive coping strategies? What would you say to his parents about their negative strategies?

I think there's a good chance Ollie will stick to his positive strategies because he feels the benefits of them. It's not difficult for him at the moment, as he's doing well at school. This could change, though, especially if most of his friends choose an unhealthy lifestyle and he ends up copying them. But I'm confident that he will stay strong and healthy and not copy the negative behaviours around him.

Can you now see positive coping strategies that Naomi, Ollie's parents and Pavel could have used instead of avoiding competition, drinking alcohol and smoking and overusing computer games?

Yes, there are many things they could try instead and it's not too late! People so easily fall into habits of things they find easy and pleasurable rather than things they find difficult and pleasurable. We need to encourage them to see all the wonderful, positive relaxation activities they could be doing to become healthier, stronger and more resilient!

CHAPTER FIVE: BUILD YOUR COURAGE

On page 126, you read about Roman, Solomon and Thalia. I said, "Roman, Solomon and Thalia are all afraid of something." Can you say what each one is afraid of, deep down? (There may be more than one thing or more than one way of interpreting it.) What would you say to each of them if you could be a wise and positive voice in their heads?

Roman has many anxieties. He's very sensitive to other

people around him and what they might be thinking. He has some aspects of social anxiety: other people make him very nervous and school is full of other people. He doesn't know whether they're his friends or not and perhaps he's too anxious to try to find out. He hates the noise and the worry about not knowing the answers. These are things that many people would be a bit worried about but Roman has developed a really big aversion to all the difficult feelings and experiences that school brings.

Solomon is a little similar in that he is keeping quiet to avoid people hearing his voice, but he isn't generally afraid of school, just speaking up. His fear, worsened by the teasing he has received, is now focused on the fact that he will need to make a presentation in class. Solomon has a specific fear.

Thalia began with a specific fear – of injuring herself again – but this has now grown into a wider fear of "what might happen?"

All these characters have fears or anxieties which are growing and this is very common during adolescence. I would tell each of them that's not their fault but there are some things they can do. Roman might need professional help because school phobia can be very hard to deal with without advice from outside the family. Solomon could tell an empathetic teacher about his genuine anxiety and the teacher should help him with some strategies to cope with doing the presentation. There will be others who are just as worried and the teacher can help, for example by pairing them up. Thalia has some very natural anxieties but really does want to go back to circus school (unlike Naomi from Chapter Four, who probably didn't want to go back to her gymnastics competitions). So, I would suggest to Thalia that she goes back and does some different activities there, to ease herself back in and build some other skills. Perhaps she will then decide she'd like to try the same activity where she injured herself: in that case, a good, empathetic teacher will help her build her confidence. Courage and confidence go hand in hand and building new and old skills will increase her confidence.

I would also suggest to all of them that they will find it easier to have the courage to face their fears if they use everything I've talked about in this book: especially building their support network, skills and coping strategies.

CHAPTER SIX: BUILD YOUR FUTURE

Do you think Kesia will apply to study medicine and Michael will apply to university? What would you tell each of them about heartsong? What other advice would you give them about their futures?

I don't know if Kesia and Michael will make those choices! I think they should if they want to and if they think they'd benefit from it. Not everyone will enjoy or needs to go to university and there are many jobs which don't require that sort of education. But taking your education as far as you can is usually a good idea because it gives you more options and opportunities. It also gives you the chance to meet a wider variety of people than you'll usually have met at school or that you'll meet in your first job. If you do it soon after school, it's a very good opportunity to have a few years of maturing and learning before settling down to a job.

But, as I say, it's not necessary for a fulfilling and successful life.

Both Kesia and Michael should speak to a careers expert who can talk them through practical possibilities. (This could be a teacher or someone from a careers advice organisation.) What they shouldn't do is be held back by their families' very specific expectations. Their parents know them well, of course, but that doesn't mean they'll make every correct judgement and they might have blinded themselves to what would really suit Kesia and Michael.

I think Kesia should keep an open mind, perhaps talking to some people who are medics and others who are in creative careers. She might be right or wrong about whether she's suited to being a doctor. But she doesn't need a creative writing course to become a writer and she should certainly look at other courses she might enjoy, as that would give her more options if she changes her mind. It's really important to choose a course you're genuinely interested in. Her parents are correct that it's not easy to make a career from writing but many people do and Kesia might. I certainly hope she carries on writing as it's a wonderful skill and hobby and can be a fulfilling career, too.

I think Michael should go for university if he possibly can! It will give him more options later and help him grow his confidence.

I'd remind them that heartsong can be found in all areas of life. The luckiest people find a job that allows them to include heartsong but most find theirs in other areas of life, such as hobbies, home, family, friends. Both Kesia and Michael are creative and that's a really good start, which will bring them loads of options throughout life.

I'd urge them to be themselves and face their futures positively and bravely and not be afraid to make mistakes. Going to university or not, taking or dropping a subject, starting or quitting a hobby, opening or closing a door: each of these things can be right or wrong. We just have to make our best judgement at the time, following our heart and our head, listening to others as well as ourselves. And we can always change direction if we find we've made the wrong choice.

RESOURCES

My own resources for well-being

Books: *Positively Teenage* covers how to look after all four legs of the table of well-being and *The Awesome Power of Sleep* and *The Teenage Guide to Stress* focus on sleep and stress.

My website is all about aspects of well-being and you'll find lots of free materials: www.nicolamorgan.com. For schools, there are teaching materials including videos, activities and the chance to have a live Q&A. On the page for *Be Resilient*, under Books, you will find links to relevant resources and teaching notes.

Other general resources for resilience

A good overview of the history of how psychologists see resilience: https://www.newyorker.com/science/maria-konnikova/the-secret-formula-for-resilience

Some good tips on building resilience: https://psychcentral.com/lib/10-tips-to-build-resilience-in-teens-and-young-adults#1

And really clear, reassuring advice on Australia's Kidshelpline: https://kidshelpline.com.au/teens/issues/building-resilience

HELPLINES

Childline: 0800 1111

Samaritans: 116 123

Young Minds: if you need urgent help, text YM to 85258 – it's a 24/7 service and is free on most networks.

FRIENDS

This is a great video explaining Dunbar's number and why 150 is the approximate maximum number of "friends" a human can manage: https://www.youtube.com/watch?v=zZF6vXMGBOw

Robin Dunbar's book on this is *Grooming, Gossip and the Evolution of Language*.

My book all about friendships, why they're important and how to enjoy them is *The Teenage Guide to Friends*. There's a chapter in *Positively Teenage*, too.

WELL-BEING AND HEALTH
Healthy eating
Good advice from the British Nutrition Foundation: https://www.nutrition.org.uk/healthyliving/lifestages/teenagers.html

Show your parents/carers this page from BBC Good Food: www.bbcgoodfood.com/howto/guide/healthy-eating-what-adolescence-need

Exercise
Advice for teenagers: https://kidshealth.org/en/teens/easy-exercises.html

More good advice here: https://www.verywellfit.com/exercise-for-teens-1229644

Sleep
I have written extensively about sleep and you will find lots of advice on my website as well as all the detail in my book, *The Awesome Power of Sleep*. There is also very useful advice for teenagers on this NHS page: https://www.nhs.uk/live-well/sleep-and-tiredness/sleep-tips-for-teenagers

Relaxed breathing
A good video about belly-breathing: https://www.youtube.com/watch?v=_xQJ2O4b5TM

Simple deep breathing exercise from the NHS: https://www.nhs.uk/conditions/stress-anxiety-depression/ways-relieve-stress/

Listen to my free relaxation audio on podcast: https://www.podomatic.
com/podcasts/nicolamorgan/episodes/2017-12-14T03_06_49-08_00
or visit my website and put "audio" in the search box.

EMOTIONAL HEALTH

Eating disorders

BEAT has excellent advice about identifying and dealing with eating
disorders: https://www.beateatingdisorders.org.uk/types

Negative thoughts and anxious thinking

You can find my Pathways Exercise on my website: https://www.
nicolamorgan.com/wellbeing-and-stress-management/positive-
pathways-brain-practical-wellbeing/

Social anxiety

Information from the US National Institute of Mental Health: https://
www.nimh.nih.gov/health/publications/social-anxiety-disorder-more-
than-just-shyness/index.shtml

CHARACTER STRENGTHS

The 24 "character strengths": https://www.viacharacter.org/character-
strengths-via

LUCK

A neat video summary of the idea behind Richard Wiseman's Luck
Factor: https://www.youtube.com/watch?v=RyZuDu2eAu4

AND FINALLY, FOR FUN:

Take a look at *The Most Magnificent Thing* by Ashley Spires. Yes, it's a
picture book, written for young children. But it's lovely and has a
strong message about being resilient. Picture books are clever because
they pack a big message into just a few words and pictures.

ACKNOWLEDEGMENTS:

This book springs organically from a tangled accumulation of wisdom and ideas from everything and everyone I've read, agreed with and listened to over my life. But if it were not for one person, it would still be tangled: my perceptive and clever editor, Alice Primmer. Thank you! You did it again.

ALSO BY NICOLA MORGAN: